The Messianic Commons

Images of the Messiah after Modernity

David Benjamin Blower

scm press

© David Benjamin Blower 2024

Published in 2024 by SCM Press
Editorial office
3rd Floor, Invicta House,
110 Golden Lane
London EC1Y 0TG, UK

www.scmpress.co.uk

SCM Press is an imprint of Hymns Ancient & Modern Ltd
(a registered charity)

Hymns Ancient & Modern® is a registered trademark of
Hymns Ancient & Modern Ltd
13A Hellesdon Park Road, Norwich,
Norfolk NR6 5DR, UK

All rights reserved. No part of this publication may be reproduced,
stored in a retrieval system, or transmitted,
in any form or by any means, electronic, mechanical,
photocopying or otherwise, without the prior permission of
the publisher, SCM Press.

David Benjamin Blower has asserted his right under the Copyright, Designs
and Patents Act 1988 to be identified as the Author of this Work

Scripture quotations are from:
New Revised Standard Version Bible: Anglicized Edition, copyright © 1989,
1995 National Council of the Churches of Christ in the United States of
America. Used by permission. All rights reserved worldwide.
Authorized Version (AV) of the Bible (The King James Bible), the rights
in which are vested in the Crown, are reproduced by permission of the
Crown's Patentee, Cambridge University Press.

British Library Cataloguing in Publication data
A catalogue record for this book is available from the British Library

978-0-334-06638-5

Typeset by Regent Typesetting

The Messianic Commons

Fresh, original and timely. I have always loved art that has to remake the world before the art can be accommodated or held. It takes a particular kind of artist to make such work, one whose gifts are in the tradition of poets and prophets. This book is one of those rare pieces of art, and Blower is one of those rare kinds of artists. The treasure that enables this remaking of the world is what he calls the messianic commons – in choosing this language he is breaking open a tradition so that it can be inhabited generously by all those who long for a better world, where all things can be made new, and seek to embody it now. He draws deeply and playfully on Jewish and Christian scriptures and indigenous worldviews, doing some wonderful theological work. It is a work of prophetic imagination. I found the air I was breathing reading the book felt free. The book embodies the ideas expressed in it. So it resists polarities, it is open and generous and not enclosed or defended, it slips the trap of offering wholesale solutions or offering judgements. It gives hints, clues, fragments, stories, practices, imaginings, and invites you in compelling fashion to join the adventure.

Jonny Baker, author of *Pioneer Practice*

In a time where there are no clear roadmaps for the shape of our society and the role that Christianity might play, the collage of ideas presented in this book gives a timely picture that doesn't lead us off-track with inauthentic linearity. For those feeling the limitations of the structures we live among, David Benjamin Blower's words offer a rich and deeply rooted companionship.

Elizabeth Slade, Chief Officer of the General Assembly of Unitarian and Free Christian Churches

Even before I came across the Jolly Roger in the text, I was convinced David Benjamin Blower – with his wild swashbuckling style, showing so little respect for conventions, traditions and the rule of law – must be a pirate. The more I read the more it became clear to me Blower is actually an honourable theological brigand, like a postmodern philosophical Robin Hood, taking back the wealth of ideas expropriated by corporate hoarders and sharing them freely with the common people who would otherwise have no access to them. *The Messianic Commons* is an invitation to sit round a table piled high with heaps of precious multifaceted truths and to sort through these luminous views of messianic community, anarchy and ecology for ourselves.

Dave Andrews, author of *Christi-Anarchy*

This is a book about power, about the need to let go of its misunderstood and corrupted forms as 'rule'; and about release into the sacred power of mutual participation in the dance of grace. At a time when radical Christian insight is ripe for reappraisal and reactivation, David Blower brings a prophetic voice that carries from beyond the desert wastes of alienation in our times.

> Professor Alastair McIntosh, author of *Soil and Soul* and *Poacher's Pilgrimage*

This is a day for new imaginings. David Benjamin Blower gifts us a feast of dialogues and sketches in radical imagination. I simply know of no one else more qualified to help us rethink who and where we are in the Western world and beyond with our entangled roots in the Abrahamic religions. These dialogues have helped me to evaluate my own Jesus Messianism deeply, thankfully and uneasily. I am confident that these sketches will positively disrupt and encourage you too. Each piece is excoriatingly beautiful, but in my view the third chapter, *The Open Ecclesia*, is particularly significant for the crucial insight it contains for re-animating the social body.

> Dr Roger Mitchell, author of *Church, Gospel & Empire*

Poetic and prophetic, subversive and inviting, gentle and urgent, *The Messianic Commons* is David Benjamin Blower at his evocative and dazzling best. Better than any artist or scholar I know, David invites me into those wild, untamed spaces where 'the anarchic breeze' of the age to come blows fresh upon my face.

> Richard Beck, author of *Hunting Magic Eels* and *The Shape of Joy*

Out beyond the limits of the modern imagination, where the promises of progress no longer ring true, there is a voice that sings of the strange kinds of hope that might still make sense. Open the pages of this book and you will hear invitations to a kind of encounter that becomes possible in the ruins of what we thought we knew. There is treasure among these ruins, memories of things yet to be, a liberation in which we are all bound to one another, an opening onto other possibilities of common life, even now, even this late in the day.

> Dougald Hine, author of *At Work in the Ruins*

This theopoetic craftwork of bricolage invites readers to think-feel their way through the ending of the Modern era and its supporting myth of progress. Even as powerful people reach for the new certitudes of a technocratic future, many experience the world as disenchanted and falling into ruin. In the pairing of grief and hope, David Benjamin Blower resonates with the deeper mythos and wayfaring music of 'weak messianic power' that is heard more clearly where the dividing walls have fallen. As he draws on Bonhoeffer, Benjamin, Scholem, St Paul, and the intuitions of folklore and indigenous knowledge, Blower reminds us that in the heart of suffering, or patience, the messianic longing is ever-present and uncontainable. The book rests on a way of repair that is anarchic, earth-wise and gently probing, resisting certain obstacles and containers, like a root reaching for the river of the Real that 'runs beneath all things'.

Dr Katharine Bubel, Assistant Professor of English and Creative Writing, Trinity Western University, British Columbia

Blower has again demonstrated, as he did with *Sympathy for Jonah*, a radically alternative and generative reading of traditions ancient and modern. He is a podcaster interviewing the two imprisoned Johns of the Second Testament; an apprentice to a wilderness imaginary; a bard playing jazz to conjure messianic flashmobs. This extraordinary 'notebook' offers a 'mosaic' of conversations for all of us who, like Peter, find ourselves trying to find warmth at midnight beside a flickering firepit in the courtyard of empire. In the genealogy of Ellul and Berrigan, Alvez and Thurman, philosopher Blower's elegant turns of phrase are a delight to read, while interrogating big ideas: the struggles between bios and zoe, ekklesia and kirkus, nomos and koinonia, craft and capital. Critically yet compassionately he unveils secular and religious modernity as a 'world pulled over our eyes', and commends a (re)turn to messianic roots. As a Christian, I love how so many of the sketches in this 'open studio' provide compelling re-readings of our Testament (especially the much-maligned Paul). Blower's symposium, curated over the last decade of music, blogging and activism, invites and animates deep excavation, courageous discernment and improvisational discipleship for those who would keep vigil with the Angelus Novus.

Ched Myers, author of *Binding the Strongman* and co-author of *Healing Haunted Histories: A Settler Discipleship of Decolonization*

The Messianic Commons throws together theory, craft and praxis into a poetic and compelling call to sacred anarchy. Blower opens up narrow cracks in Christian tradition through which we can glimpse, perhaps, the messiah.

> Dr Marika Rose, Senior Lecturer in Philosophical Theology, Winchester University, and author of *Theology for the End of the World*

From the prologue and opening pages contrasting the ideas of Bonhoeffer and Benjamin, to Gershom Scholem's messianic anarchy, indigenous writers, and the multitude of biblical texts and linguistic shifts we've made to our detriment over the millennia, Blower weaves a fascinating, convincing and heartfelt tale that is worth listening to. This is a postmodern take on modernity, poetically written and immersed in messianic imagination and anarchy, comprising fragments and making valuable connections that might be ignored or lost otherwise. In this book, Blower's brilliant, polymathic mind and deeply compassionate heart come to the fore, impressing upon the reader that the idea of messianism is fuelled by a deep and desperate hope for a better world, a hope that Blower writes is 'so close to grief that one might easily be mistaken for the other'. Inevitably, the reader will go away with more questions than answers, which is the difficult yet still fulfilling way of wisdom that Blower invites us to travel.

> Dr Jayme R. Reaves, Co-ordinator at the Centre for Encountering the Bible, Sarum College, and author of *Safeguarding the Stranger*

Blower describes the treasure he seeks to share as 'fragments'. In *The Messianic Commons* he lavishly gives away all the treasure he has discovered, uncovered and recovered – these disruptive and creative new takes on the old messianic contours of anarchy, ecology and the margins. In doing so, he prepares a table that is somehow roomy enough for those who need room to question, as well as those who need room to put down deeper roots.

Blower's great insight is that the messianic imagination is at once ancient and ever new, both disruptive and creative. He shows us in these fragments that we don't have to choose between being either deconstructors or protectors of our traditions. Rather, a third way is possible. It begins by sharing the treasure we have in common through the messianic imagination and the wager to 'live (now) in order to arrive at the sort of world we would like to live in'.

> Sam Ewell, author of *Faith Seeking Conviviality*

Contents

Prologue viii
Introduction and Acknowledgements xi

1 Religion Is Strange Again   1
2 Messianic Folklore   12
3 The Open *Ekklesia*   37
4 All Things   57
5 Sacred Spaces   76
6 Transfiguring Work   95
7 The Sacred Absence of Rule   113

Bibliography   132

Prologue

A story is told of a potter who became renowned for the beauty of her vases. They were made in a mosaic fashion, from broken pieces of all sorts, and yet the fragments were set together in perfect tessellation. No one could understand how she found one perfectly fitting piece after another.

The emperor was stirred by her work and began to fill his palace with one vase after another. He would occasionally ask her how she made them in such perfect tessellation, and she would change the subject, until, one day after some wine, she revealed her secret. It was by going to the lands that the emperor had laid waste in conquest that she was able to gather so much broken pottery, enough to create any form she pleased in perfect tessellation, one after another.

It is said that, in his latter years, the emperor sat for long hours with the vases, in silence.

Introduction and Acknowledgements

I'm not sure when I became so acutely haunted by the messianic idea, or how it happened. Nobody else around me talks this way, though my friends, adversaries and correspondents have mostly been very accommodating. In any case, this constellation of visions has only sketched itself thicker with time and reflection.

This is a book of fragments, for three reasons.

The first reason is that most of the chapters were written first as notes and reflections after gatherings, dialogues and symposiums on one subject or another. With many voices around the table or the fire, or trapped in boxes on a computer screen, the ideas moved in strange clouds according to their own whims. Things are not so linear. I've gradually come to see a wilder ecology of thought as a good thing, and so one reflection follows another, with the names of various friends and associates scattered through the pages. None of these gatherings were on the subject of messianism, I will add. They were about anarchy, or craft, or forms of association, or enclosures, or labour and wealth. The common thread of messianism is the story that continued to assert itself in my own thoughts.

The second reason is because a compelling coherence sang loudly from the gathered pieces, but there was no score to read and there were no maps to follow. Perhaps it is best this way. I have been wandering among these themes to discover something. I'm not relaying a neatly bound system of ideas, already drawn up and nailed down.

The third reason is due to the nature of the subject matter. This is not the kind of 'knowledge' that wishes to be regimented in a linear fashion. It is a constellation of interrelated things. You try blowing your whistle and commanding them to line up in order of height. I don't believe these things work that way. The media theorist Marshall McLuhan favoured the mosaic style of writing, in which the pieces might produce interesting new results if read in a different order. There is naturally some repetition of themes here, but, I hope, always from slightly different angles of illumination.

*

All that remains is to acknowledge the following people whose thoughts have fed into these pages, whose advice has been valuable, and whose friendship and hospitality have made this book possible, such as it is. There should always be more names than there are but, in any case, my thanks go to Lydia Catterall, Paul Milbank, Vanessa Chamberlin, Mike Love, Roger Mitchell and Sue Mitchell, Miles Irving, Spencer Thompson, Julie Tomlin, Andy Knox, Jon Blower, Mike Gilbert, Annie Dimond, Rosa Blower, Jesse-John Blower, Azariah France Williams, Elysia Willis, Stephen Backhouse, Danielle and Joel Wilson, Stephen Blower, Elizabeth Oldfield, Anna Bjorkman and Dougald Hine, Stefan Skrimshire, Hannah Malcolm, Elizabeth Slade, Linda Woodhead, Mike Winter, Rina Atienza, Sam Ewell, Susie Poole, Christian Cogley, Paul Wenham and Andy Proudfoot.

I

Religion Is Strange Again

Two Surrenders

Once upon a time, two men sat writing letters. They wrote what they wrote during the Second World War under not dissimilar circumstances. One of them scrawled in the quiet moments snatched while fleeing across Europe from the Nazis. The other wrote from his prison cell in Germany. In a time of catastrophe and endings, when all kinds of dormant truths were being violently exposed, they wrote with that strange clarity that only rarely emerges. They predicted the present.

There's something deeply enigmatic about these two epistles. They seem to call out to each other across the valley in deep resonance. But they also seem to run in contrary directions. 'We are proceeding towards a time of no religion at all,' wrote one. 'Men as they are now simply cannot be religious any more.'[1] Meanwhile the other conceded that all our best efforts to rid the world of the intellectual embarrassment of religion had amounted to nothing but smoke and mirrors, and that theology secretively underpinned all the workings of the world whether we liked it or not.

*

The first was Dietrich Bonhoeffer, the German Protestant pastor and professor of theology, who was imprisoned by the Nazis for his involvement in the resistance movement. In spite of his pacifist leanings, he had been party to an assassination attempt on Hitler. There in his prison cell, in his last days, he finally conceded to Modernity what religious people had been resisting for generations. 'The world has come of age,' he admitted.[2] All efforts to press the world back into the naive childhood of religion were pointless. The Enlightenment had shown that God was no longer needed as an explanation for the world. Everybody knew that the crops still grew, whether you went to church or not. Christian apologetics fought an embarrassing and ridiculous losing battle. The more scientific mysteries were solved, the more the ground shrank under the feet of the Christian God. And while the world was tearing itself apart with such violence, Bonhoeffer wondered, 'Is it not true to say that individualistic concern for personal salvation has completely left us all? Are we not really under the impression that there are more important things than bothering about such a matter?'[3]

There's something poetic about granting Modernity its gains, just at the disastrous twilight of that era. As soon as Bonhoeffer names the thing and honours its truths, it seems to immediately turn and depart. What Christian apologists failed to do with a million fiery arguments, Bonhoeffer does with one quiet relinquishment.

All this raises many questions but, of course, the question on Bonhoeffer's mind was what this would mean for Christianity. 'The linchpin is removed from the whole structure,' he says. 'If we had finally to put down the western pattern of Christianity … If religion is no more than the garment of Christianity … then what is a religionless Christianity?'[4]

*

The second writer was the German Jewish intellectual Walter Benjamin, who wrote his *Theses on the Philosophy of History* while fleeing from the Nazis, sending copies to friends as he went. The opening thesis describes an odd picture: a sort of robot dressed in Turkish attire with a hookah pipe, sat at a chessboard. The robot appeared before the world as an early miracle of artificial intelligence. It could win a game of chess against any human opponent.[5] Benjamin was referring to the Mechanical Turk, a technological spectacle invented in the late 1700s. It toured Europe for almost a century, beating nearly everyone at chess, including Napoleon and Benjamin Franklin. But the miracle machine was, in the end, revealed to be a fraud.

RELIGION IS STRANGE AGAIN

An expert chess player would be hidden beneath the table the whole time, operating the robot mechanically. Benjamin saw in this story a parable about historical materialism – the Marxist idea that material inequalities must eventually arrive at an equilibrium. Or, as Martin Luther King famously put it, 'The moral arc of history is long, but it bends toward justice.'[6] Historical materialism is like the chess-playing robot, says Benjamin. It wins every time, but only because theology is secretly hidden below, pulling the strings. In other words, Modernity's hope to arrive at utopia, Marxist or otherwise, without the aid of religion was a fraud. Religious ideas and energies ran under everything.

Benjamin mirrors Bonhoeffer's thoughts here, in the shape of relinquishment and confession. The religious imagination was coming to terms with the painful truth that Modernity really didn't need God as an explanation of anything. Meanwhile, the secular imagination was coming to terms with the painful truth that it couldn't function without religion, theology, folklore and myth, even if these dubious energies are 'wizened and [have] to keep out of sight'.[7] Benjamin was a Marxist thinker, so the question on his mind was what this theologically charged world meant for the revolution.

*

Modernity runs onward anyway, 'like a watch ticking in the pocket of a dead man'.[8] Benjamin's religious turns are still something of an embarrassment to some,[9] and Bonhoeffer's questions have found no good framework to hold them, compelling as they are. When a paradigm collapses, there's nearly always an aftershock of movements attempting to reanimate what's died. The brief New Atheist movement tried to double-down on the certainties that Benjamin denied, and the waves of Christian apologetics defending a faith rooted in Modernity are always going on somewhere. But even so, something has come to an end. The world is changed.

*

Although the pronouncements of Benjamin and Bonhoeffer appear to run in opposite directions, they don't seem to be at odds. They run in opposite directions, toward each other, as though they might meet in the middle. They both wander away from a hubris of certainty. One leaves the comforting certainty of a world view without room for unknown religious quantities. The other gives up on the certainty of religion, proclaimed as comforting fact into the gaps of science. Meanwhile, the impervious cultural divide that kept these irreconcilable certainties separated and civil has become porous. It's not religion or secularism that collapses but the antagonism between the two. The dividing wall that kept everything separated for so long has gone. Suddenly everything is sloshing together.

*

Writing at their two bleak tables, neither correspondent seems to feel hopeless about what might lie beyond collapse. Really, they both had more immediate problems: the sort that make it a little easier to jettison pointless baggage. They were both, perhaps, fey with a little too much truth.

Bonhoeffer sounds quietly energized by his visions of religionless Christianity. The world's coming of age, he says, 'was an abandonment of a false conception of God, and a clearing of the decks for the God of the Bible, who conquers power and space in the world by his weakness'.[10] Or later: 'Now that it has come of age, the world is more godless, and perhaps for that reason, nearer to God than ever before.'[11]

Benjamin finds a mix of consolation and audacity in what is left behind in the wake of disenchanted progress. Through a willingness to experience the sufferings of the present in solidarity with the neglected histories of oppressed ancestors, liberating possibilities emerge. Benjamin sees some kind of messianic life that might interrupt the dull, homogeneous, linear rule of the powers that be. He envisages a stick in the wheel 'to bring about a real state of emergency',[12] 'to blast open the continuum of history',[13] to establish 'a conception of the present as "the time of now" which is shot through with chips of messianic time'.[14]

And though they do indeed sing from very different hymn sheets, there is a striking resonance between their respective visions. For Bonhoeffer, the end of religion meant the end of an era of individualistic private spiritualities, geared toward pleasant afterlives and indifferent to worldly realities. He envisaged a religionless Christianity as 'participation in the suffering of God in the life of the world', or 'allowing oneself to be caught up ... in the messianic event'.[15] Benjamin likewise saw a hope that was located not with power but with suffering: 'The oppressed class itself is the depository of historical knowledge ... as the avenger that completes the task of liberation in the name of generations of the downtrodden.'[16] There is, meanwhile, a corresponding rejection of the conventional paths to victory through force: 'Whoever has emerged victorious participates to this day in the triumphal procession in which the present rulers step over those who are lying prostrate.'[17] As Benjamin saw it, 'we have been endowed with a weak messianic power', with which we navigate victories and defeats.[18]

Both, in surrendering a religious certitude of one kind or another, let go of the power games of the age. Both hear the music of the messianic myth calling faintly from the places of weakness. In contrast to the demure and quietist religious categories of Modernity, messianic ideas have always been concerned with the wholeness and joyousness of material life. Messianic ideas have always resisted the powers that divide and diminish material life. These two correspondents saw a world materially enchanted with messianic imagination, located in the experience of the suffering.

*

When I read Bonhoeffer's letters years ago, I knew I'd discovered an articulation of the questions I wanted to dwell with. When I read Benjamin a few years after that, I discovered a kind of hope so close to grief that one might easily be mistaken for the other, and yet this was the sort of hope that seemed absolutely necessary. These two letters from the closing curtain of Modernity run though all that follows here.

Religion in the Global Village

> There have been many more religious men than I who have not made even the most faltering steps in this direction. Once I began to move in this direction, I began to see that it had profound religious meaning. I do not think it my job to point this out. For example, the Christian concept of the mystical body – all men as members of the body of Christ – this becomes technologically a fact under electronic conditions.[19]

Speaking just two and a half decades after Bonhoeffer and Benjamin, Marshall McLuhan sounds like a cartoon character. The world had turned into a post-war consumer capitalist fairground, lit up and strung together with an explosion of new technologies. The Western individual forged over the course of Modernity had been thrown into a paradox. On the one hand, all were further individualized, newly endowed with the freedom to create a bespoke self by going shopping. On the other hand, everyone was being wired up to everyone. Everything was everyone's business. The world was re-tribalizing. New energies were shrinking the world into a global village. The rather managed and curated 'peace' of 1945–2000 – the short-lived boomer paradise – was an unsustainable fantasy. In its padded keeping, we would forge the cities, languages, technologies and epistemologies from which we would be obliged to face dystopias approaching over the horizon.

Obviously, no sensible person thought to interpret this new situation as a religious one. McLuhan had an odd capacity to view the world as though he had just arrived there from somewhere else, with a host of unexpected and rather medieval comparisons up his sleeve. Electronic humanity as the body of Christ certainly perplexes all theological sensibilities, and yet the extraordinary advent of our new inter-connectivity does carry profound religious meaning. The old empirical boundaries between this and that are passed over without a second look these days. Boundaries between one and the other, between sacred and secular, between your thoughts and mine, between my religion and your lack thereof, between this history

RELIGION IS STRANGE AGAIN

and that, between that war and this peace ... all the old borders are just a few rotten fence posts now. The old filing system that kept things orderly is in chaos, causing joy and panic in equal measure. Religion has become strange again.

*

One outcome of the global village was the discovery that most people are quite religious after all. The sense that humanity had outgrown such things was a feeling that belonged to a European experience of the recent past. The world has since been shaken up like a snow globe. Not only is the world of today a religious place, it's also religious in all kinds of ways that the modern Western category of religion doesn't really have the stomach to digest.

Nationalist border-anxiety is one inevitable reaction to the passing of an old structure that divided the world up in a certain way. The loss of control, the exposure of every epistemology to the weather in a world of global involvement, is so terrifying that elections are now fought over how many rubber dinghies are crossing the English Channel.

*

The modern conception of religion was forged in the school of divide and rule. Religions were thought of as mutually exclusive, without overlap. They were mythic narratives competing against one another to colonize the afterlife. Here was a category formed in the image of its creator, if ever there were one. Today's religious imaginations don't fit the mould at all. Innumerable, porous, political and earthy; they're obliged to describe themselves with language from elsewhere.

*

The US theologian William Cavanaugh notes that the term 'religio' very rarely appears in the literature of the Middle Ages.[20] This is because whatever we now package up in that term was, back then, simply at large and utterly ubiquitous. The capturing of that imp, that spirit, was a miracle of the early modern imagination. It had run on too long and caused too much mischief, and so, finally, it was gathered up, filed and indexed within Modernity's library of empirical knowledge, where it would be subservient to the state.

Today, it's hard not to feel the comedic irony in that turn of events. Religion was tamed and caged as a sort of superstition. It was newly understood to the enlightened eye as a commonly held fiction that gives structure and form to life, a sense of safety and a rule of responsibility. All this was sealed up in a jar in deference to the state, which is today seen in exactly the same way.

*

In the not so distant past, nothing could be more niche, and no room quite so closed, as a room full of Christians discussing theological matters over coffee and cake. Today, we live in a world where religious communities are deconstructing their own world views, while Marxist atheists and Jewish historians are writing tomes on the apostle Paul.

*

The false peace of the late twentiethth century has gone awry. The debts are stacked up. In October of 2019, I stood, with my collaborator Vanessa Chamberlin, in Trafalgar Square amid the throng of an Extinction Rebellion protest. The Red Brigade, in their eerie attire, walked slowly through the crowd and everyone was silent. And then, at the top of the steps, a voice began to read from the book of Revelation, while everyone stood and listened. A queue of readers took it in turns until they had read the whole thing. The crowd were of no faith and of many faiths. The text belonged to no one and to everyone. It was being given away, returned perhaps, to the soil and the suffering. This scene isn't new. It's old. The imp is loose again. Folk religion and political activism are synonymous again.

*

Meanwhile, old-time religion of the sort Bonhoeffer had rather given up on makes its return, partly in the service of pseudo-nationalistic anxieties about the loss of 'Judeo-Christian values', and partly for lack of a deep root that would make slow moving sense in a chaotic situation. Meanwhile, religious institutions are emptied out and overwhelmed all at once. Meanwhile, wars are religious again. Meanwhile, atheists pray and Christians do atheism for Lent. The world finds itself called to the land, and called back to the symbols of eras before colonial Modernity. The world finds itself called again to the religious symbols of Modernity itself, which awakens to defend itself, and called to the strange prayers of thinking machines full of nihilist grief and humour. The world finds itself called to the forgotten prayers of indigeneity, to enquire of the ancestors how we might yet become good ancestors.

I don't wish to romanticize or advocate for the strangeness of the present. That would be ridiculous, like advocating for the weather. It's everything all at once. It doesn't belong to anyone. It's not on my side. It's not on your side. But in the interest of predicting the present and thinking together in the now, all this has a bearing on these sketches of the messianic commons.

Moving the Tables

My friend Sam Ewell envisaged the radical priest Ivan Illich ever wandering between two tables, a table of theologians and a table of social scientists.[21] These worlds were kept quite separate in Illich's day, in the late twentieth century. One had to give some explanation for how these two spheres were to be to be understood, if ever they were to run into each other. We don't seem to need explanations for this any more. In fact, we are scratching our heads trying to explain why we once felt we needed to explain this. As the strange new world of universal involvement begins to normalize, the normative past begins to look strange. Here we are, on our feet, leaning this way and that way between the two tables. And here we are, moving things around into one big table. And here we all are, leaning in with our best ear and all our loose change.

*

THE MESSIANIC COMMONS

There's a danger in setting a table for everyone, in that we might not really talk about anything at all. Or worse still, that in trying to be all things to all people, one becomes a universal charlatan. For that reason, I'll begin by owning the soil of my own imagination. I am a Christian, and I speak from the Christian hill. I suspect some might take the false impression that I would like to distance myself from this soil, but this is quite untrue.[22] I don't want to do that at all. Some will object that I'm throwing out too much treasure from the Christian stores. But I don't want to throw anything away. I want to give everything away. What could be more Christian than to empty oneself? Christianity began as a messianic cult, but messianism is a far bigger idea than mere Christianity. And whatever messianic treasures lie forgotten in its keep, these don't *belong* to it, as property held against others. Even Christianity may occasionally have to wander out of its own city gates to remember where the Messiah makes camp.

From the earliest days of the messianic movement that swept up around that figure, Jesus of Nazareth, the messianic treasures have naturally been in the keeping of the Jewish faith tradition. This particular sect within Judaism chose to do an odd and costly thing. It chose to give away the messianic treasures for free, without demanding that anyone should convert to their religion. They discerned that messianism was something that lived and moved freely across boundaries of religion and no religion (a religionless Judaism, we might say). This is a gesture toward a similar thing. This is a common table set to give away the messianic treasures across boundaries of difference. This is a breaking open of the religious enclosures, an opening up of messianic commons in a moment when religion has become strange again.

I've learnt, perhaps, more about messianism from people who aren't particularly religious. The messianic imagination naturally wanders free of religious categories these days. It's time for a universal garage sale. The table is set for whoever.

Notes

1 Bonhoeffer, *Letters and Papers from Prison*, p. 91.
2 Bonhoeffer, *Letters*, p. 108.
3 Bonhoeffer, *Letters*, p. 94.
4 Bonhoeffer, *Letters*, p. 91
5 Benjamin, *Illuminations*, p. 245.
6 Dr Martin Luther King, 'Remaining Awake through a Great Revolution': a speech given at the National Cathedral, Washington, DC, 31 March 1968.
7 Benjamin, *Illuminations*, p. 245.
8 Stearn, *McLuhan Hot & Cool*, p. 308.
9 Lowy, *Fire Alarm*, pp. 19–20.
10 Bonhoeffer, *Letters*, p. 122.
11 Bonhoeffer, *Letters*, p. 124.
12 Benjamin, *Illuminations*, p. 248.
13 Benjamin, *Illuminations*, p. 254.
14 Benjamin, *Illuminations*, p. 255.
15 Bonhoeffer, *Letters*, p. 123. Notably he references here the Hebrew tale of the suffering servant from Isaiah 53.
16 Benjamin, *Illuminations*, p. 251.
17 Benjamin, *Illuminations*, p. 248.
18 Benjamin, *Illuminations*, p. 246.
19 Stearn, *McLuhan Hot & Cool*, p. 302.
20 Cavanaugh, *Theopolitical Imagination*, p. 32.
21 Ewell III, *Faith Seeking Conviviality*, pp. 105–31.
22 'By no means!' as Paulos would say. And 'their condemnation is deserved!' he would say (Rom. 3.31, 3.8). Moments of messianic fervour tend to generate alarming and paradoxical situations that get all the heckles up.

2

Messianic Folklore

Human creatureliness seems to carry a kind of nostalgia for things that have not yet been; dim memories of futures; fantasies about the world over its horizon. We are creatures that long, or lengthen. Plato concluded that our intuitions about what is to come must be conditioned by memories formed before we came into the world.

Collectively, these longings take shape in political movements, which feel toward the world as we variously dream it, and also in religious institutions, which give story and form to our intuitions. Between the old poles of religion and politics, there runs something like folklore – messianic folklore – mythologies that call from both past and future. Here are stories humming with possibility, moving around the rocks of what is happening.

Messianic claims about the shape of the future can be made by any fool. They're a dirty business, enlisted in all kinds of power play. Even so, if we lean into the music of messianic folklore, I believe we'll find something quite free of all powerful interests. A dim image that calls to the subjected, the outlawed, the powerless and the feral.

Two Wagers

Here is a tale of two stories. One is the story of eternal life. The other is the story of the age to come. These two siblings of the religious imagination have vied with one another, converged and diverged at different times and in strange ways. To understand the messianic idea, one must get a feel for where one story ends and the other begins.

MESSIANIC FOLKLORE

I grew up on the story of eternal life, as I suppose many Christians did. 'Whoever believes in him may have eternal life,' it says.[1] This was a story about the good afterlife. Jesus was the figurehead of the Christian religion, and to be a Christian meant to go to heaven when you died. This is a fine story but not a messianic one. The Messiah comes to redeem the world itself.

The Greek words commonly translated 'eternal life' in John's Gospel are *zoen aionion*. They actually carry a very different idea. There was never a less controversial New Testament scholar than F. F. Bruce, and in his commentary he clarifies: 'this means the life of the age (aion) to come',[2] which, as he later says, is to be 'established on earth'.[3]

Here is the second story – the life of the age to come – buried there under the first. This is the messianic idea in Judaism, the hope of a colonized people. In this story, the present world longs toward a dawn that will bring it to liberation, rest and wholeness, to fullness of joy and the end of its subjection to deathly violence.

But *zoen aionion* was translated by Jerome into Latin as *vita aeternia*, which, in the late Middle Ages, became *euerlastynge lyfe*, and then finally *eternal life*, as it was put in the old King James version. It's easy to see how it went where it went, but the meaning is not the same. There's a fork in the road of language here that has led to contrary ideas.

The life of the age to come tells of another time but not another place. It happens here, in some future. Here is precisely the subject of its happening. Here is what matters. Eternal life, on the other hand, is generally envisaged as another place but not another time. Eternal life is going on somewhere else right now. It's the abode of the righteous dead, and we are to hope that we will join them there, in that somewhere else.[4]

The divide between these two stories is, in fact, strange and porous and full of trickery. They're not mutually exclusive. They roll into each other in all kinds of ways. For now it is enough to say that when the religious imagination of eternal life recovers the dangerous memory of the life of the age to come, something autonomous and frightful awakens. Something leaves the old masters and begins to gamble the present away in all kinds of mischief.

*

Here is a tale of two wagers, corresponding to our two stories.

I heard about Pascal's wager as a child, long before I knew who the French mathematician and physicist was. It was an idea that had trickled down into popular Christian apologetics. The wager goes like this: if I live as a Christian and it turns out that it's not true after all, I will enjoy my life and when I die, I will lose nothing. But if you choose not to be a Christian and it turns out to be true, you will lose everything.[5]

This wager belongs to the story of eternal life but not to the messianic idea of the life of the age to come. It's a creature of Modernity and it chimes with that era in several ways. For one thing, it's very individualistic. It's entirely concerned with the outcome for oneself, in a sort of unnatural isolation. Old Christian wisdom says, 'Love doesn't insist on its own way.'[6] Is it really by isolated self-interest that we map the paths to redemption? For another thing, the wager is coercive. It blurs consent. It asks us to capitulate on the strength of a veiled threat: we might regret it or we might not. There would be something almost playful about it if the stakes were not so high.[7]

I don't know if the German philosopher Theodor Adorno had Blaise Pascal in mind when he wrote it, but the final maxim of his *Minima Moralia* sounds like an alternative wager; a messianic wager on the life of the age to come, if you will. 'The only philosophy which can be responsibly practised in the face of despair', he says 'is to contemplate all things as they would present themselves from the standpoint of redemption ... as it will appear one day in the messianic light.' He adds at the end, almost mirroring Pascal, 'the question of the reality or unreality of redemption itself hardly matters'.[8]

This wager is not individualistic. The life of the whole community is at stake; both the human and the more-than-human. Our liberation is bound up with the liberation of all things. It is a vision of all things reconciled that the messianic imagination longs toward.

MESSIANIC FOLKLORE

There's no coercive trickery. It's not tribal: it's ethical. It doesn't ask us to convert or die. Rather, it asks us how we would live in order to arrive at the sort of world we would like to live in. There is no demand for religious capitulation, only an invitation to anyone who would live toward their best imagination of the world.

Perhaps the messianic grace reaches back to meet us as we reach forward in our various hopes. Perhaps redemption becomes a reality. Or perhaps it doesn't. Either way, Adorno calls the messianic wager the only responsible way to live.

*

Does Adorno's messianic wager carry better prospects for a person's happiness than Pascal's? It depends on what makes a person happy. In one sense, I doubt it. A commitment to the redeemed life and peace of all things might well lead a person into all kinds of jeopardy, not to mention a certain dis-ease with the present. On the other hand, many would think it the happiest of paths, to be broken open for the life of the world and the wonder of all things.

*

Adorno's wager isn't really a religious proposition. We might think of it not so much as a wager but as a thought experiment. The experiment is expressed in three moves.

First is a question. How might the world appear to me if the messianic dawn finally arrived and all was healed and whole and as it longs to be? What does my gut reach for or envisage? There is a shadow side to this question. My answer reveals to me what I believe is wounded or askew or wrong with the present.

The second move is a humbling. I don't judge the world from outside. I am part of it. I am part of whatever wounds and brokenness and incompleteness I perceive, and even more that I don't perceive. My hopes and judgements are themselves certainly incomplete and possibly very wrong. There's no objective knowledge among creatures. What is the posture that embodies this smallness, this encounter with limit and doubt?

THE MESSIANIC COMMONS

The third move is a sort of resolve. In my knowing smallness, with some healthy doubt in one hand, I set my course toward the best vision I have anyway. In the end, the best vision I have is the best path I can walk.

*

Adorno's thought experiment requires no religious confessions or affiliations. It sounds a rather secularized and disenchanted sort of messianism. And yet something of the wager remains, at least. It has to. It remains open, ajar, to the unknown possibility of the messianic dawn. It is the folklore-ish open edge to the answer from without that gives messianism its porous innerlife, and its ever unfolding ecology.

To exclude the possibility of the messianic event is to claim a total knowledge of the situation, and knowledge is power. They who claim the knowledge become the cutting edge of progress, managing redemption for everyone else. The same thing occurs when the messianic event becomes absolutely known, domesticated and colonized by one religious group who think they know all its secrets. The endgame can't be owned by any one terrestrial party, 'so that none can boast',[9] or rule, or exert force, or control outcomes. In other words, the Messiah remains wholly other. Where the otherness of the messianic disappears, all that is left is religious triumphalism and the colonial winds of despoiling progress. These are strictly *anti*-messianic (or anti-Christ as the New Testament puts it), in that they themselves appear *in place of* the messianic.

*

In the letters of Paul, messianic imagination was something practised 'through a glass, darkly'.[10] The looking glass of the ancient world wasn't, in fact, glass but very well polished metal. The image one saw was a dim and warped reflection of things. This, to Paul's mind, was the kind of seeing we were capable of, and it was best we remembered it. We should note that this practice of imaging, in prayer or thought, was not done by looking through a glass into another world, but by looking into a strange reflection of this one; not into an other-worldly eternal life but to a this-worldly life of the age to come.

The obscurity and otherness of this imaging practice, checks the boasting of any one group or the rise of any one story. Redemption is not managed by a hierarchy. What we encounter instead is something more like anarchy.

Messianism and Anarchy

The Israeli philosopher and historian Gershom Scholem once described messianism as 'a kind of anarchic breeze' in the well-ordered house of Judaism.[11] Amid the Jewish communities of medieval times, a conservative emphasis on the keeping of religious law – the *halakhah* – was a matter of survival for this marginalized and vilified group embedded in Christian lands. Through the keeping of their law, they kept the integrity and coherence of their story alive. And so those who harboured utopian messianic leanings were considered something of a disturbance, since they tended to be rather more loose on the subject of law. Scholem writes:

> There is an anarchic element in the very nature of messianic utopianism: the dissolution of old ties which lose their meaning in the new context of messianic freedom. The total novelty for which utopianism hopes enters thus into a momentous tension with the world of bonds and laws, which is the world of *halakhah*.[12]

In other words, law seems to lose its meaning before visions of a world made whole, where whatever we might call 'wrong' is just no longer possible. In this respect, the messianic imagination is anarchic because it reaches toward a space beyond law. Messianism longs for anarchy. It has the ability to imagine the mystical, the fantastical and apparently wholly unrealistic vision of a world that is absolutely free, and yet without moral shadow.

*

If Christian theology had ever noticed what Scholem described, or at least paid attention to Scholem himself when he described it, it might have been able to break away from the anti-Semitic twine that has held it in such monstrous and costly contortions. From the earliest times, the New Testament's dichotomy between law and faith was interpreted by non-Jewish devotees as a comparison between Judaism, which they judged was a religion of law, and Christianity, which they called a religion of faith (though the meaning of that word continues to be elusive). Meanwhile, the Judaism Scholem describes contains the dichotomy between law and messianic anarchy within itself. Paul's critique of law is an integral dynamic of Judaism, not an outsider's anti-Judaic hatchet job. An awareness of this anarchic breeze within Judaism might help us to better understand the enigmas and paradoxes of the New Testament that a certain brand of theologians have poured over with gnostic reverence. Perhaps histories of crusades, pogroms and holocausts might have been avoided, though I'm inclined to think that theological ignorance is the result of a lust for power, and not the other way around.

Meanwhile, Christian religious institutions are buried in their own sorts of law and the anarchic breeze has been shut firmly outside. Whether or not the Christian tradition has any capacity for messianic imagination will be discussed later.

*

By one reckoning, the opposite of anarchy is hierarchy. We might envisage the workings of a hierarchy as a walled city with a tower rising high from its centre. Inside the tower sits the sovereign: the king or the queen, the first minister, the president or the chairman or what have you. There they are in grand finery. Outside the tower are the ordinary folk who, it is said, accept the rule of the sovereign because it is the sovereign who has encircled them with the protective walls they rely on for security. It is the sovereign who keeps them safe by management of their resources and labour. It is the sovereign who keeps law and order. The tower separates the sovereign from the ordinary. The wall separates the managed and known from the chaos of the unknown outside by means of law. Law is impossible without hierarchy. Hierarchy is formless without law. We tolerate hierarchy only because we find ourselves in need of law. The messianic imagination envisages the end of both kinds of management. The first-century adherents believed the Messiah figure had 'abolished the law'[13] and that the powers and rulers of the age were 'doomed to perish'.[14] All hierarchical distinctions between one group and another were ended.[15] These forms of management by laws of division would finally give way to a reintegration, a reconciliation of all things, 'so that God may be all in all'.[16] Why? Because the management of life by sovereignty and law were understood to be temporal and passing things; something we did for a time to reduce suffering in a suffering world. The messianic imagination looks back, as it were, on the present age with its laws and powers, as a precarious, tottering construction of matchsticks. To contemplate the present in the light of this folklore is to ask: how might these divisive measures be removed without causing disaster? Where to begin gently liberating the world, and in what way?

A complete answer to this question can never come from within the scenario. It's always a yard beyond. Even so, it is the messianic task to make paths in the light of the question. The question is ours. And this is hope: that the answer may reach back to meet that which lives the question in good faith.

*

I recall hearing the US author and podcaster Keith Giles talking about the ills of the Scofield Bible and its alarming end times tropes, which have held sway over the American evangelical imagination.[17] Jesus is an odd messianic figure, having two arrivals, one in the past and one in the future (though this is not unique). The second coming of the Messiah is imagined by some in the light of these rather developed end times narratives. They don't anticipate the end of hierarchy and law, but a doubling down on both. In this vision, the law and rule of the Christians will prevail, followed by their escape from the world that is consigned, with its populace of outsiders and backsliders, to disaster and misery.

In the light of such a story, it's perhaps quite natural that Giles chose to flip the script and declare that *we* are the second coming of Jesus. This way, the grim threats associated with the Scofield Bible's second coming are mercifully defused.

Here, we see one kind of certainty replaced by another. One says, 'the Messiah is coming any time now and he is our boy, not yours. You can be sure that the events will unfold as we have pronounced.' The other says, 'I am the coming of the Messiah, and there is no answer or event to anticipate besides me and what I choose to do.'

In either case, the messianic imagination has collapsed because the otherness of the messianic is wiped away. The Messiah's comings and goings are either announced, programmed and wholly owned by one particular group for whom the Messiah is more or less a team mascot; or else the Messiah has no comings or goings or autonomy of any kind, apart from the actions of the group who declare themselves to be the Messiah. The result is the same in either case: both groups claim total messianic authority by wholly absorbing the messianic otherness into their own keeping and control. Both parties act as managers of the messianic. Both presume to act 'in place of', and so anything we might properly call messianic is gone.

Christendom managed the Messiah in both ways at once: by acting as managers of the second coming and by assuming its authority in the meantime. Power absolutely must neutralize messianic imagination, precisely because power cannot coexist with its anarchic breeze.

*

It's not difficult to see why we might recoil from such folklore. The messianic imagination is a place where questions gape painfully unanswered, where sufferings wait unhealed, where stories wander incomplete. It remains and abides with sufferings and longings. It forms imperfect and tangling paths in the light of experience. It contemplates the *eucatastrophe*, the possibility of redemptions beyond our own asking and imagining.[18] Meanwhile, the Messiah remains wholly other and

MESSIANIC FOLKLORE

wholly autonomous of all our imaginings. The Messiah belongs to no party.

*

When the classless society didn't materialize in the early twentieth century, some Marxist thinkers began reflecting on the messianic roots of the philosophy. Marxism was, as Benjamin described it, secularized messianism. But the messianism from which the theory was formed was absorbed into the theory, into the historical process. It became something like the idea of progress. In this respect, the Left mirrored the Right. The final outcome and the pathway to it would both be mapped and managed from the ground.

Messianism is apophatic. That is to say, it rests on what is unknown and doesn't try to gain mastery over it. We can collaborate toward our best images of redemption, and this is a world-making task, but these images of redemption are always partial. They always come from our smallness, our various standpoints. Any whole knowing is always obscure, seen through a glass darkly.

There is something almost trickster-ish in the messianic. Our longing toward redemption is good, is sacred, is kind, is wholesome. But wholeness and full knowing are always a yard further. This is a loving withdrawal. It is this that Modernity loathed and tried to destroy with colonizing knowledge.[19]

*

Messianism leads toward anarchy because it leads away from those two kinds of rule. It moves away from law, toward where transgression is no longer possible. It moves away from rulers, since a hierarchy is no longer required to uphold the law that is no longer of service. To try to absorb and manage and programme the messianic is to stand in place of it. This generates more law and more rulers. For this reason messianism is so easily killed by its inheritors, like a butterfly nailed to a board and kept behind glass. But how, on the other hand, to stay with the trouble? How to resist the controlling grip? To keep one's mind and balance while abiding in this knowing unknowing is an art or, better still, a creaturely wisdom.

Messianism and Ecology

The Italian philosopher Giorgio Agamben describes a Hebrew Bible from the Middle Ages. In its pages, there's a depiction of the feast at the dawn of the messianic age, where the humans have animal heads. 'It is not impossible', says Agamben, 'that in attributing an animal head to the remnant of Israel, the artist of the manuscript ... intended to suggest that, on the last day, the relations between animals and men will take on a new form, and man himself will be reconciled with his animal nature.'[20]

*

While eternal life came to be associated with a disembodied great beyond elsewhere, the life of the age to come is concerned with all that is here, with the redemption of our embodied lives and the redemption of the great body of the earth, of which we are part. For this reason, strange visions of bodily resurrection fill the messianic imagination. In the life of the age, the picture of redemption is terrestrial and earthy.

An anthropocentric view sees the living planet as the stage on which the drama plays out. All that is not human is reduced to a backdrop for the action. It is a quite different thing to see the living planet, the material creation itself, as the subject of messianic redemption. This re-roots the sacred imagination back into *adama*, back into the soil. Human liberation is tied to ecological liberation because humans are literally made of the soil, the humus. The human creature is not external to the ecological plains we walk our compasses over.

*

Law and hierarchy tend to divide things up. This map of divisions has shaped our ecological imagination wherever progress and modernity thrive. Nature is strictly other, outside the walls of civilization. We are apart from it. We defend ourselves against its chaos. We torture it for its secrets. We extract its resources, colonize and subdue it. It is savage and incomprehensible because it has no law.

This fever dream does as much violence to us as it does to the rest of nature. Agamben calls these projects of separation 'the anthropological machines'. The matter at hand, he says, 'is of understanding how they work so we might eventually be able to stop them'.[21]

The progress myth compulsively divides and separates, filing and categorizing everything in its well-managed index of empirical knowledge. Messianism is anti-progress. It reconciles all things. The anarchic breeze is ecological. It hovers where ecology is arighting itself from the divisions imposed on it.

*

Messianism is thoroughly materialistic. On the other hand, the messianic itself must always be an unknowable reference point, other and autonomous and beyond the sphere of ecological all-ness. This might have the appearance of a paradox because western thought has tended to express itself through arguments between its usual schools of wizardry: secular materialists versus religious apologists. Indigenous cultures everywhere see no paradox or tension between the material and the spiritual, for want of less beleaguered words. They're not mutually exclusive realms. There is no intrinsic argument between them.

*

Hierarchies and laws create inner circles of privilege and margins of exclusion. The more-than-human world finds itself an oppressed party in the outer realms. The scene is a tragicomedy. The human oppressors are themselves ecological members who pretend not to be. In ecological time, the project is absurd and brief and hopeless. The humans of progress are beginning to look like bandits who've barricaded themselves into a house.

The earliest messianic discourses in the Jewish tradition reflect deeply on this sorry theatre. Redemption is certain. Gentleness inherits the earth in the end. Belligerent power certainly destroys itself. It passes like the grass of the field. For this reason, unspectacular waiting becomes a cornerstone of early messianic thought: the very focused and intentional practice of not participating in the war to take control of the situation.[22]

What comfort may be drawn from the long waiting game depends on how deeply we associate and identify with the ecological whole, which certainly outlasts all despoiling progress. This is a story bigger than ourselves and it invites us to loom in God's time.

*

The first-century messianic communities believed that the more-than-human creation also had capacity for messianic imagination. They saw the living planet continuously humming in prayerful longing for liberation, since it found itself sorely subjected. The earth was in constant, wordless prayer, and they sought to join in with it. Here was a mystical practice of transgressing the divide between themselves and the rest of creation. A re-rooting themselves.[23]

*

A world beyond hierarchy and law is unimaginable to the mind shaped by human history and progress. But what we find unimaginable, the more-than-human world practises without effort or even thought: unmanaged life. It grows all around us and yet we can only touch this vision by a flex of mysticism.

*

My friend, the writer Dougald Hine recalls the thought of his friend Paul Kingsnorth, who keeps fish in a tank and quickly learns how much management and expense is involved in maintaining an environment that keeps fish alive. All this, says Kingsnorth, 'a river or a lake does for free and with ease'.[24]

*

These sketches in messianism take the shape of a triangle. The first point is anarchy and the second is ecology. The third point, below, is marginalized life. This is the shape of good trouble.

Messiahs and Margins

In the Jewish Talmud, the school of Rabbi Sheila tells us the name of the Messiah: 'Shiloh, as it is written, "until Shiloh come".' But then the school of Rabbi Jannai tells us the Messiah is actually called Jinnon. And then the school of Rabbi Channinah says that the Messiah's name is, in fact, Chaninah (note the dropped 'n').[25] The Talmud offers many suggestions regarding the identity of the Messiah and the nature of the messianic age – its length, the generosity of its redemptive reach, the geographical locations associated with its advent, and so on and so forth. The suggestions are numerous, various and often at odds with each other. All this carries the humility, humour and seriousness of folklore and a kind of wisdom about how to live well in a web of different hopes and experiences and standpoints. We tend to envisage redemption in our own images and to call it by our own names, but humility and humour know that redemption itself is quite free of all these.

*

I must take with good humour that the Rabbis of those times were oddly unanimous on the subject of Jesus. It was said that this messianic figure could not be the Messiah, though he is often welcomed in, these days, as 'a great son of Israel'.[26]

Reflection on my own tradition raises a question. How to draw upon this messianic figure, without collapsing into the adversarial mascot-hype that, as described above, strikes me as very un-messianic? This question begs another: can Christianity be, properly speaking, messianic? Some will wonder how Christianity could possibly *not* be messianic. What is Christianity, after all, if not an oddly prevalent messianic sect?

The difficulty is a question of time, posture and power. The rabbi and scholar Abraham Cohen puts it simply: 'Whereas other peoples of antiquity placed their golden age in the dim and remote past, the Jews relegated it to the future.'[27] We will need to ask ourselves some questions. When is our golden age? What is our posture toward it? Where does the power gather itself?

*

THE MESSIANIC COMMONS

The theologian N. T. (Tom) Wright has done more than most to restore something messianic to the Christian imagination. And yet he makes an interesting case on this matter when he imagines himself in dialogue with the Jewish intellectual Walter Benjamin. In 1940, Benjamin found himself travelling across Europe to flee the Nazis, finally committing suicide to evade capture. It was on this journey that he wrote his brief and fascinating *Theses on the Philosophy of History*, a tract on the messianic threads running under Marxism, on disenchanted progress as the belligerent song of the oppressor, on the unrecorded sufferings of the oppressed, and on the weak messianic power that everyone carries as a sort of reflection of the dim possibility of redemption. 'The Jews were prohibited from investigating the future,' he said. 'This does not imply, however, that for the Jews, the future turned into homogeneous, empty time, for every second of time was the strait gate through which the Messiah might enter.'[28]

For Wright, Benjamin is too despairing. He has 'pushed all the weight of expectation onto the future'.[29] Rather than staring into the bleak uncertainty ahead, which reliably disappoints, 'the apostle Paul', says Wright, 'spoke precisely of the messianic event which had *already* declared God's judgment against all the forces of evil, and God's vindication of his suffering people.'[30] Benjamin should look backward into the sure ground of the past, not squint into the uncertainty of the future. Well, here is the question of time and privilege that concerns us.

*

The New Testament is an intensely messianic collection of texts. It is awkwardly poised in future anticipation. Everything is groaning toward the future event. Everything is lining itself up for The Day, when the strong will be thrown down from their thrones and the poor lifted up.[31] 'How long!' pray the saints, in the book of Revelation,[32] which ends with the invocation, 'come lord, come'.[33] Even when the Messiah walks the earth in the present, he speaks of the future when the Messiah will come.[34]

Quite naturally, the further a tradition walks through time, the more it refers backwards to the events on which it built its house. We all walk into the future backwards. Gradually, the Messiah is confined and domesticated in the past, and redemption becomes *vita aeterna*, an afterlife mystery, off to the side.[35] They who look ahead risk despair.

Wright's quarrel with Benjamin is to some degree a restatement of an age-old disagreement between Christian and Jewish traditions.[36] It is the Jewish side that speaks from the margins. The messianic leaning toward the future stands with what is now suffering. It is attuned to what is incomplete and unknown. It speaks from the crushed edges of life. Messianic cults have generally been religions of the oppressed and the colonized. They emerge among people whose lot in the world evokes longing for altered and arighted futures. This is certainly the ilk of the New Testament, which catalogues the thought, the folklore, the rituals, the sufferings and the ecstasies of a community whose glimpses in the present fuelled future hopes for liberation from colonizing powers and the end of despoiling tyrants.

If the Christianity that wandered on from that unsustainable fervour wanted to be messianic again, it would need to open at least one hand to the uncertainty of the future. It would need to temper its certainties and its total ownership of the Messiah it knows from the past, with apophasis – with an openness to the Messiah who has not yet made themselves fully known. It would need to rediscover itself, not as a catalogue of answers but as a collective prayer awaiting an answer. It must reckon with the reality that the resurrection of one remains an incomplete messianic event until it becomes materially meaningful for all. This leaning toward future anticipation is always a relinquishment of knowledge, which is to say a relinquishment of power, and an openness to the sufferings of the past, the present and the future.

*

The loss of messianic imagination in the Western Christian tradition correlates with its migration from powerlessness to power, from the place of the oppressed to the position of colonizing rule. Eusebius, a fourth-century bishop of Caesarea, wrote a history of the first Christian emperor, Constantine. His posture toward the Jewish experience became a common trope. From the triumphal halls of Roman imperial might, he wrote about the 'the calamities that immediately after their conspiracy against our Saviour overwhelmed the entire Jewish race'.[37] Eusebius insinuates that the Jewish people were colonized, conquered, destroyed and crucified in the thousands (by the Romans, of course) because they refused to become Christians. Their sufferings are not a wrong to be arighted but the just outcome of their *own* stubborn wrongs.

To the ruling powers, those who remain in messianic anticipation are a problem because they await the overthrow of the powers themselves, and a future beyond management. They who hold power wish to see the glorious struggle in the past alone, since it was that struggle that established their rightful rule. They resist the future event because they wish to see themselves as the conclusion of the story. If others suffer, it can only be that they have failed to accept the victory of the past, which is already won, finished and completed. There are no problems to solve, only outsiders who refuse to accept their solutions.

The loss of messianic imagination in the Christian tradition is apparent in its widely held assumption that the world will be redeemed insofar as it capitulates to the Christian religion. If the messianic event is in the past alone, and the Christians have become its managers and gatekeepers, the world must now answer to the Christians.

*

To be properly messianic is to displace redemption from oneself.

I have no doubt that even the Christian story, of which I am part, is capable of messianic imagination: wherever it is able to relinquish power and privilege, wherever it finds itself amid the experiences of suffering and incompleteness, and wherever it relinquishes a controlling grip on the image of redemption, which remains demonstrably hidden from view.

The hiddenness of the messianic is absolutely in keeping with New Testament sensibilities, even if it would seem to be a heretical betrayal to established Christian power. Is the Messiah not hidden among the suffering?[38] Is our redemption not hidden with the Messiah?[39] Is liberation not hidden, and thus waiting to be revealed?[40] Is not the whole thing brooding over an extraordinary hiddenness that is awaiting a great *apocalypsis*, a great revealing?[41] The hiddenness of the Messiah, the messianic secret, and the ongoing possibility of encountering it where you never knew it might be hidden, make the bones of these texts.

*

Giorgio Agamben has recently popularized the language of messianic time. There is a time between the resurrection of the Christian Messiah and the resurrection of everything, and this time represents a sort of overlap, a stirring of chronological time. The ending has appeared in the middle, and yet it is still to come, since everything still hurts.

On the one hand, I find myself suspicious of the idea. There is much leisurely sophistry, talking artfully about time, but what difference does it make to the suffering and the marginalized, to the earth locked down under concrete and to the lengthening queue of extinctions? At its worst, it is used to wax on a kind Christian triumphalism, which is deaf to all that longs and hurts. The problems are solved but they're not solved, and yet again they are!

On the other hand, it is a vision that seems to point to something true: there are glimpses of the age to come all around. The skies declare it. The hawthorn is free of all law and all rulers. Laughter, *eros*, kindness and feasts everywhere declare it. Perhaps such visions of the future, appearing rooted in the present, liberate us from feeling inescapably trapped under the powers of the present age. Perhaps this mixing of the times enables us to break things up and to be participants; to embrace what Benjamin described as our 'weak messianic power'.[42]

*

Scholem tells an old messianic tale that dates back to the second century. It's a story about the Messiah who has in fact already come, but who 'waits in hiding'. In this vision, the Messiah is presently living outside the gates of Rome 'where he dwells among the lepers and beggars of the eternal city'.[43] Here is a story that speaks to our questions of power, suffering and time. Perhaps the messianic is indeed among us but in waiting, hiddenness and marginal obscurity. Further still, the medium of story (and this tale has been retold in many variations) speaks of the generative space between what is known, what remains hidden and dormant, and the generative weave of sharing and storing our visions in our common complexity.

Progress and Messianism

Messianic cults and their religious traditions are naturally at risk of absorbing the messianic into themselves and claiming to be the fulfilment of messianic rule, being certain of their own imminent triumph and vindication. The European progress myth is a secularized extension of this hubris. History is seen as one linear story and it belongs to those who win the power to tell it. They're history's conclusion or its cutting edge. Always the triumphal procession goes forward to better and better things, and always in the hands of the victors.

*

Walter Benjamin's *Theses* pulse with the impossible longing that not only the future but also the sufferings of the present and the past must be somehow redeemed. In the well-known ninth thesis, the angel of history looks back over all that has happened with longing, but something is wrong:

> His face is turned toward the past. Where we perceive a chain of events, he sees one single catastrophe which keeps piling wreckage upon wreckage and hurls it in front of his feet. The angel would like to stay, awaken the dead, and make whole what has been smashed. But a storm is blowing from paradise; it has got caught in his wings with such violence that the angel can no longer close them. The storm irresistibly propels him into the future, to which his back is turned, while the pile of debris before him grows skyward. The storm is what we call progress.[44]

Such is the march of the victors who rush forward to fix the world. It is costly to stay with the trouble, to be with the suffering and live with the uncertainty of our limitations. There is a certain anxiety that underlies the aspirations of the *Ecomodernist Manifesto*, 'to use humanity's extraordinary powers in the service of creating a good Anthropocene'.[45]

*

Attempts to conjure decisive solutions to the problems and predicaments of history reliably result in the domination of one story over others. The Western progress myth becomes blind, or perhaps chillingly indifferent, to the sufferings of other stories. It is captured by the assumed superiority of its own narrative as the story of salvation.

Wherever the messianic imagination is thus co-opted, whether in the religious realm or the secular, or indeed both, the result is the rule of one group who freeze history in their own image. The recovery of messianic imagination involves its rewilding, its relinquishment to a realm of otherness, and a horizontal reconciliation and re-integration of complexities.

*

In the story of the sheep and the goats, the Messiah welcomes those who had fed him, clothed him and visited him in his sufferings and imprisonments. But these people had no recollection of ever having met him. It turns out that messianic redemption had not been in the keeping of any one superior group, but had been hidden all along amid the suffering.[46]

This makes an instructive contrast with Giles' messianic proposals. Giles suggests that the Messiah has returned and is present in Giles himself, and in all of us who so identify. The Messiah has returned in the first-person plural, as a designated 'us'. In the story of the sheep and the goats, however, the Messiah is indeed hidden among us, but always in the second-person, always in the other; further still, the Messiah is always in the suffering, marginalized and criminalized other, who is found outside and beyond the self-designated carriers of the story.

Open Messianism

It is said that messianism has a price. Jacob Taubes, who was Scholem's student, noted that rabbinic Judaism tended to suppress what was regarded as too much messianic fervour. They saw it as a dangerous foray into history, and perhaps it is just that. How does one sustain such longing and anticipation without wearing down the mind and the soul? Sometimes it's a matter of survival to collapse into a hubris of certainties. There is something to be said for a gentle and fixed contentment amid the incompleteness.

*

Donald Trump, the forty-fifth US president, became a messianic figure. He appealed, in part, to marginalized groups whose fortunes he promised to reverse. He was hailed as 'the Lord's anointed' by his supporters (and the word 'Messiah' means, literally, 'anointed one'). He was associated with prophecies and the language of end times trumpets, in the hope that he would redeem a degenerating historical situation. All this, largely, within Christian circles. This tells us so many things.

*

Messianic fervour naturally reaches its highest and most unwieldy pitch at moments of historical crisis, change, collapse and renewal. At best, it creates spaces where brave and generous imagination opens new paths into futures that are otherwise closed by the present state of things. At worst, it becomes a rallying cry of denial, a cult of hero worship or a hotbed of tribal thuggery. Groups that become fixed on their own closed outcomes are routinely destroyed or poisonously embittered by the reality of an unmet vision, or by the life wasted on endless adversity.

It's also true that longing is a kind of pain, and I have no wish to romanticize a meandering malcontent with the present. Languishing hopes weary the heart.

*

MESSIANIC FOLKLORE

'Tromos kai ekstasis,' says the US theologian Ched Myers, referring to the ambiguous original ending of Mark's Gospel, in which the resurrected Jesus makes no appearance.[47] 'This poignant dialectic of trauma and fear on one hand, and ecstasy on the other ... It's a perfect dialectic for anyone who dares to hope for a better world. You're constantly traumatized by the way the world is, but also animated by this ecstatic vision of the way the world could be.'[48]

*

Taubes suggests, against his old teacher Scholem, that in order to survive itself, the messianic idea must go inwards at some point. 'Every attempt to bring about redemption on the level of history without transfiguration of the messianic idea', he says, 'leads straight into the abyss.'[49]

Messianic visions are unreasonable and unrealizable. They can never be forced into being. The outcome is always disappointment, disaster, death and despair. In order to keep one's mind, the messianic imagination has to stay in movement, stepping bravely into the fray and then regathering inwardly as a sort of incomplete prayer before stepping out again. It must be in movement between the internal and the external, between the shared and the individual.

*

Taubes' word of caution is well noted here. Movement inward and outward helps the group or the individual remain supple and complex. It saves busy hands from a sick heart. It calms the pride of overly fixed ideas about the shape of redemption. It gives a second place to stand when the first becomes untenable.

While Taubes suggests movement between the inner and outer, these sketches suggest another kind of movement to keep the messianic imagination alive and generative, present, loving and rooted in good faith. This is the horizontal movement between groups and people of difference. Redemption by this approach must remain incomplete, obscure, always partly hidden from view, seen only through a glass darkly. This means that it remains open, horizontally, to the witness of all experiences, longings and sufferings, and that it doesn't crush itself into the interests of any one group or story. This also means that it remains open, beyond the horizon, and that redemption remains other and autonomous. This is an open messianism: a world-making activity around a table of difference.[50]

*

'The story is circular!' says Myers.[51] When the women of Mark's Gospel find themselves confronted with the incomplete story of an empty tomb, they are told by an angelic being to go back to where they began, to the backwater of Galilee. They are to return not as all-knowing colonizers of the future but as disciples once again – that is learners – of the longing and incomplete present.[52]

*

There is a posture here of smallness that delivers us from madness and tyranny on the one hand, and from withdrawn indifference on the other: 'the little road' as Dougald Hine calls it.[53] 'You are not obligated to complete the work,' say the rabbis, 'but neither are you free to abandon it.'[54]

This leaning toward the future paired with a refusal to claim an authoritative knowing of it, will likely strike some Christian sensibilities as a rather impious withdrawal. I would consider it a deepening of messianic faith.

There is an old story. The Messiah once came and people began to ask him about the coming day of redemption, which still remained oddly absent besides a few glimmers. All the hearers were shocked by the Messiah's reply, that even the Messiah, in fact, did not know.[55]

Notes

1 See John 3.16.
2 Bruce, *The Gospel of John*, p. 89.
3 Bruce, *Gospel of John*, p. 265.
4 Here's Bonhoeffer sketching the divide: 'What do I mean by "interpret in a religious sense"? In my view, that means to speak on the one hand metaphysically, and on the other individualistically. Neither of these is relevant to the Bible message or to the man of to-day. Is it not true to say that individualistic concern for personal salvation has almost

completely left us all? Are we not really under the impression that there are more important things than bothering about such a matter? (Perhaps not more important than the matter itself, but more than bothering about it.) I know it sounds pretty monstrous to say that. But is it not, at bottom, even Biblical? Is there any concern in the Old Testament about saving one's soul at all? Is not righteousness and the kingdom of God on earth the focus of everything ...? It is not with the next world that we are concerned, but with this world as created and preserved and set subject to laws and atoned for and made new' (*Letters and Papers from Prison*, pp. 94–5).

5 Pascal, *Pensées*, pp. 121–5.

6 See 1 Corinthians 13.5.

7 Bonhoeffer considers this sort of religious coercion pointless, ignoble and unchristian. 'Pointless, because it looks to me like an attempt to put a grown-up man back into adolescence, i.e. to make him dependent on things on which he is not in fact dependent any more, thrusting him back into the midst of problems that are in fact not problems for him any more. Ignoble, because this amounts to an effort to exploit the weakness of man for purposes alien to him and not freely subscribed to by him. Un-Christian, because for Christ himself is being substituted one particular stage in the religious ness of man, i.e. a human law' (*Letters*, p. 108).

8 Adorno, *Minima Moralia*, p. 247.

9 See Ephesians 2.9.

10 1 Corinthians 13.12 (AV).

11 Scholem, *The Messianic Idea in Judaism*, p. 21.

12 Scholem, *Messianic Idea*, p. 19.

13 Ephesians 2.15.

14 See 1 Corinthians 2.6.

15 See Galatians 3.28.

16 1 Corinthians 15.28.

17 Keith Giles, 'Ending the End Times', *Nomad* [podcast], N264 (9 January 2022), https://www.nomadpodcast.co.uk/keith-giles-ending-the-end-times-n264 (accessed 26.9.2024).

18 J. R. R. Tolkien's term for 'the good catastrophe, the sudden joyous "turn" ... It does not deny the existence of *dyscatastrophe*, of sorrow and failure: the possibility of these is necessary to the joy of deliverance. It denies (in the face of much evidence, if you will) universal final defeat and in so far is *evangelium*, giving a fleeting glimpse of Joy, Joy beyond the walls of the world, poignant as grief' (*Tree and Leaf*, p. 68).

19 The medieval anchoress Julian of Norwich saw that a part that remained hidden from her: 'It is the Lord's private matter, and it is the royal prerogative of God to be undisturbed in that which is his own business. It is not for his servant, obedient and reverent, to pry at all into these secrets. True, our Lord has pity and compassion on those of us who busy ourselves therewith. Yet I am sure that if we realized how much it would please him and benefit ourselves to refrain from this, we would stop' (*Revelations of Divine Love*, p. 107).

20 Agamben, *The Open*, p. 3.

21 Agamben, *Open*, p. 38.
22 See Psalm 37.
23 See Romans 8.18-26.
24 Hine, *At Work in the Ruins*, p. 145.
25 Cohen, *Everyman's Talmud*, p. 347.
26 Buber, *Two Types of Faith*, p. 9.
27 Cohen, *Everyman's Talmud*, p. 346.
28 Benjamin, *Illuminations*, p. 255.
29 Wright, *Paul and the Faithfulness of God*, p. 1483.
30 Wright, *Faithfulness of God*, p. 1483.
31 See Luke 1.52.
32 See Revelation 6.10.
33 See Revelation 22.20.
34 See Matthew 24.44.
35 Wright, for his part, consistently leans very much toward *zoen aionion*, rather than *vita aeternia*.
36 Scholem, on the other hand, says this: 'The Church was convinced that by perceiving redemption in this way it had overcome an external conception that was bound to the material world, and it had counterpoised a new conception that possessed higher dignity. But it was just this conviction that appeared to Judaism to be anything but progress. ... What appeared to the Christians as a deeper apprehension of the external realm appeared to the Jew as a liquidation and as a flight which sought to escape verification of the Messianic claim' (*The Messianic Idea*, pp. 1-2).
37 Eusebius, *The History of the Church from Christ to Constantine*, p. 31.
38 See Matthew 25.31-46.
39 See Colossians 3.3.
40 See Colossians 3.4.
41 See Romans 8.19.
42 Benjamin, *Illuminations*, p. 246.
43 Scholem, *The Messianic Idea*, p. 12.
44 Benjamin, *Illuminations*, p. 249.
45 Hine, *Ruins*, p. 104.
46 See Matthew 25.31-46.
47 'So they went out and fled from the tomb, for terror and amazement had seized them' (Mark 16.8).
48 Ched Myers, 'Easter and Empire', *Nomad* [podcast], N294, 6 April 2023, https://www.nomadpodcast.co.uk/?s=n294 (accessed 26.9.2024).
49 Taubes, *Cult and Culture*, p. 9.
50 I'm indebted to my friend Mike Love for this image.
51 Myers, *Binding the Strongman*, p. 399.
52 See Mark 16.4-8.
53 Hine, *Ruins*, pp. 158-9.
54 *Pirkei Avot* 2.21. This text is a collection of ethical Mishnaic texts that were compiled in the third century CE.
55 See Matthew 24.36.

3

The Open *Ekklesia*

The Gathering

Ekklesia is the Greek word commonly translated 'church' in English New Testaments. There it stands, like a youth hoping to escape a dull parent. An *ekklesia*, meaning 'a gathering' or 'an assembly', could be a cohort of devotees or it could be a rioting crowd. For the Greeks, the word was political, harking back to the emergence of Athenian democracy. The *ekklesia* of Athens was a gathering in which citizens (excluding women and slaves, who were not recognized as citizens), would come together to discuss whatever was at hand; where each, in theory, had an equal voice and a stake in the path ahead.

The word 'church', on the other hand, leads to a different set of ideas. While an *ekklesia* was a civil gathering, the word church is unambiguously religious. It can be traced back via the Germanic *kirk* to the Greek term *kyriakon*, which means 'lord's house'. A *kyriakon* is a specific place, a building, a temple to one lord or another. An *ekklesia* is not a specific place at all but rather a space. It's not even a permanent space but rather an event, a happening. An *ekklesia* is a convergence of beings. It appears and disappears fluidly. It is a moot, a flash mob, a riot, a session. It's a gathering for cards, whisky and strong opinions. It may appear in one place and then reappear quite differently somewhere else. It may be organized or it may be spontaneous. It might be an assembly of religious devotees or it might not, but it is certainly a gathering of citizens who converge to make space for the voice, for the enspirited tongue, of each participant.

*

THE MESSIANIC COMMONS

The choice of those first-century messianics to self-describe as *ekklesia*, and not as *kyriakon*, is fascinating. They passed over the language of temples in favour of a more political description; indeed, a more fluid and uncontained description. However, they didn't take the term *ekklesia* as they found it. First, they appealed to a concept of citizenship that bore no allegiance to any ruler, authority or power. It was an anarchic citizenship in the ancient nomadic tradition of the Hebrews, similar to that of the Arabian Bedouin, as Jacob Taubes describes:

> Israel shares common ground with Arabia, where there is a similar tendency to rebel against any forms of human authority. The Bedouin tribes in particular, the desert nobles, share this characteristic belligerence against social order. They are organized into a 'community without authority,' in a similar fashion to Israel's theocratic community. A Bedouin chief never calls himself a king; at the very most he can be *Said al Arab*, a spokesperson for the Arabs. According to an early Islamic viewpoint, God alone is worthy of having dominion over mankind. A human *mulk*, a monarch, would be anti-God.[1]

The language of 'heavenly citizenship' was not an abdication from all that is earthly and material, but rather an abdication from all subjection to earthly kings and caesars, whose business was, and is, the enclosure and exploitation of all that is earthly and material.

More still, unlike Athenian democracy, there were no exclusions from citizenship across gender or social status. It was a thing the world had not seen before: an *ekklesia* of women and an *ekklesia* of slaves. From the outside, the spectacle was disturbing and ridiculous. The second-century critic Celsus looked upon them and saw only a cultish movement made up of 'the foolish, dishonourable and stupid, and only slaves, women and little children ... wool-workers, cobblers, laundry workers, and the most illiterate and bucolic yokels'.[2]

*

Very quickly, this movement of radical gatherings went even further. Having naturally emerged as a sect within Judaism, it ruptured beyond its bounds. It did so almost against its own better judgement. This new movement of messianic *ekklesiae* became a religiously diverse network of gatherings. Here was something that has always proved difficult to contrive by design: complex space. It was so alarming in its own time, even to its own participants, that the controversy generated half the New Testament texts, and its shadow haunts the other half likewise.

The memory of these complex spaces remains so strange that they have been theorized and theologized into something more sensible. That brief window of complex space was an event. Perhaps it wasn't something that could be sustained in a controlled fashion. It collapsed out of the other side into a new religious homogeneity, from Jewish to Christian. Christian theology has spent most of two millennia describing this homogenization as the goal those extraordinary complex spaces were always reaching for. It was only ever meant to be a migration of God from the Jewish religion to the Christian one. Those primitive *ekklesiae* were absorbed retroactively into a homogeneous Christian imagination. The *ekklesia* was renamed the *kyriakon*, the church. It was rebranded under the language of temples.

So then, the *ekklesia* is a religiously diverse gathering. The *kyriakon* is a religiously homogeneous one.

*

'The Pauline question whether circumcision is a condition of justification is to-day, I consider, the question whether religion is a condition of salvation,' wrote Bonhoeffer from his prison cell.[3] The closer he came to facing God, as they say, the braver his religious thought became. Perhaps it is not the fear of God that keeps us in check after all.

As a child, I found it odd that I would hear so many hours of sermons dedicated to an ancient controversy regarding a religious ritual performed on a boy's wand at eight days old. It was the distinguishing mark of Judaism, and it became the boundary over which a religiously diverse *ekklesia* would begin to host its gatherings. It was never said that Jewish messianics should desist from circumcising their boys on the eighth day. By no means. It was said, however, that people would be recognized as members of the messianic *ekklesia* whether they were circumcised or not. Those early Jewish messianics chose, at considerable cost to themselves, to open this kind of complex space. They broke bread with others without demanding religious conversion. In fact they dissuaded it. They argued fiercely against any pressure to convert. They considered the whole idea a totally un-messianic kind of power play, a sort of cultural imperialism. Judaism remains quite disinterested in converting the world to itself.

The gradual tipping counterwise into a new religious homogeneity was certainly more than complete by the time of the Nicaean Council, when Constantine declared that the Christians should 'have nothing more in common with the Jews, who are our adversaries'.[4] Constantine was the slamming gate, the enclosing Christian 'no' to that generous Jewish 'yes'. Since then, Christian rhetoric has tended toward the untruth that the Jewish messianics of the first century eschewed their ancient rite of circumcision altogether, along with all their ancestral law, as though uncircumcision were in fact a requirement of religious salvation. This falsehood is an enclosure of complex space. When we look for enclosure, we will see it everywhere in many forms.

*

There is a curious instance in the epistle of James where we find the word 'assembly' used for once, rather than 'church'.[5] We might assume that the word *ekklesia* has here been translated literally, but not so. In fact, the Greek word beneath this translation is not *ekklesia* but *synagoguen*. It would certainly not have felt right to translate this word as 'church', but the translators chose not to render the word *synoguen* as 'synagogue' either. This word remains hidden under different word: a mark of the retroactive Christianizing of a religiously diverse *ekklesia*, a purging of the scandal of complex space.

What if we allow that movement to be what it really was: not *kyriakon* but *ekklesia*, a network of complex messianic spaces? What if we suspended our assumption that messianic *ekklesia* is the business of one enclosed religious tradition? What if this liminal happening were seen to occur across such boundaries and outside of them altogether? What if we saw complex messianic spaces, not as a saviourist strategy or the next big thing, but as a vital condition for life, arighting and reaching toward its wholeness? If we did, we would encounter a startling possibility: that the *ekklesia* is a happening that belongs to no particular group, is closed to nobody, and may well occur in all kinds of unexpected spaces. It may be happening, somewhere else, right now, among a gaggle of very different people.

Numinous Ruptures

Now to wild and uncontaining things, to what the howling Pentecostals call the Holy Ghost: in Greek, *tou hagiou pneumatos*, the Spirit of Otherness, the *Pneuma*.

Complex space feels dangerous to all parties. No one wants to take responsibility for what might occur here. In New Testament tales, the buck is always passed to the *Pneuma*. 'The *Pneuma* made me do it,'[6] says Peter, after eating with the enemy. Gentle old Peter was as reluctant as any to cross religious boundaries and social taboos. No one wants to be the weak link. It was only because he was taken up in visions from the *Pneuma*, and had heard the voice of God telling him to eat from a platter of defiling heathen foods. Only for these reasons did he accept the invitation to go and eat with the uncircumcised Cornelius, who was, worse still, a Roman centurion. Peter may have been somewhat softened by his dwellings. It is said that he'd stayed some days with a leather worker whose workspace was, no doubt, a defiling dungeon of dead animals and the human urine that was used to condition the leather.[7]

This was a moment of religious rupture. As Peter awkwardly tells his messianic tales to the Roman villa of uncircumcised colonizers, the room is swept up in numinous ecstasies and singing tongues. He and they find themselves meeting over an awkward threshold. Something has changed. They are suddenly sharing complex space, pulsing with a common embodied numinous experience. What happened next was Peter's call. He initiates the heathens into the messianic sect because, as he explains when he returns to his own group, '[the *Pneuma*] ... made no distinction between them and us'.[8]

This is not a theory to be practised, this is a story about a happening. Theory came after the event. Theology came as a sense-making activity, after a homogeneous religious space ruptured into complex space. So it goes with the uninvited winds of change. Everybody dances or rages or praises or spits feathers, but it's not a theory that can be practised or criticized. Theory happens only after the event because everyone is anxious to know what is happening.

*

The *Pneuma* is a character in these messianic dramas. The *Pneuma* is a sort of benign trickster, an event, an expression of divine violence. The *Pneuma* is that dear friend who must always push the mystery red button. The *Pneuma* is the otherworldly deity who asks no permission, gives no warnings and offers no explanations. The *Pneuma* is the cloud that engulfs the world and suddenly everything is in alarming flux. The *Pneuma* is the sleeping gargantua on whose back we quietly live our lives until, one day, they awake and shake us all into the air.

*

Pneuma is the God of all things in migration.

When ancient Israel's nomadic tribal era was replaced by an era of kings in palaces, God, the nomadic tent-dweller, broke the old law by migrating as *Pneuma* into a stone temple, filling it with an impenetrable cloud.[9] When the era of kings in palaces collapsed, the *Pneuma* migrated out of the temple, let it burn, and settled in refugee camps by the rivers of Babylon, quietly haunting the colonizers' courts. In the first century, with Judaism on a threshold of collapse and rebirth, the *Pneuma* migrated once again. The *Pneuma* is characterized by migration across the laws, boundaries, thresholds and taboos of the collapsing past. The Spirit moves across when we half know this is needed, but none of us dare to do it.

*

THE OPEN EKKLESIA

The first-century messianics saw the *Pneuma* in the image of glossolalia: a God of bizarre appearance, a root system of burning tongues.[10] The *Pneuma* not only appears as tongues but is also manifest in the life of the community through their own speaking and groaning tongues, in the strange and potent exercise of their own voices. All is glossolalia; all is tongues.

In the image of tongues, the exercise of language, *Pneuma* moves in a twofold fashion. On the one hand, the *Pneuma* makes us comprehensible. We understand the stranger and the stranger understands us. On the other hand, the *Pneuma* makes places of sameness incomprehensible among themselves: we find ourselves woefully misunderstood within our own groups, by our own parties. These two alarming effects mark the fertile chaos that turns everything and everyone upside down in moments of paradigm shift. It is the tongue, the speaking voice between one and another, that burns down the house.

The first of these ideas is well known and reliably cited by those who would like to conquer the world by conversion. When the *ekklesia* is first enspirited in visions of fiery tongues, they find themselves miraculously comprehensible to crowds of travellers. First by diaspora Jews, from whom they were divided by language, and then by uncircumcised Romans, from whom they were divided by religion, culture and political allegiance. The comprehension of tongues is not a one-way street. Cornelius is able to comprehend Peter's messianic tales but Peter, to his alarm, is also able to comprehend the colonizing heathen Cornelius in return. This two-way comprehension will rattle both their worlds.

The second thing is not so well understood nor very much loved. It was irksome to the messianics that while the *Pneuma* worked miracles of comprehension across boundaries, these spiritual ecstasies would in fact cause wearying confusion within communities of sameness.[11] There is a primitive telling of this in the myth of Babel, where a group who seek to enclose themselves in a castle against the world are non-violently ruined when God goes down and confuses their mono-tongue. They suddenly become incomprehensible to one another. The hierarchical chain of command breaks down and the tower is abandoned, half-built. They're scattered over the face of the earth. They are saved, against their own better judgement, from the prison of sameness and restored to the abundance of complexity.

Both of these numinous effects are partly destructive. Both traumatize an existing social body. When we find ourselves drawn to the experience of the other, we know there may be a price to pay within our own tribe. We're likely to find ourselves somewhat distanced from those with whom we have shared the village well. The call outward is always costly.

*

In numinous times, the homogeneous group will tend either to fracture or to defensively bunker itself into withdrawn obscurity where it functions something like a time-capsule, preserving long buried eccentricities. Both paths carry loss. Both carry treasure. It's best not to despise either.

*

Ivan Illich saw the root of numinous rupture in the story of the good Samaritan, which he believed introduced to history a totally new possibility.

> In antiquity, hospitable behaviour, or full commitment in my action toward the other, implies a boundary drawn around those to whom I can behave in this way. The Greeks recognized a duty of hospitality toward *xenoi*, strangers who spoke a hellenic language, but not toward the babblers in strange tongues whom they called *barbaroi*.[12]

Illich read through archives of sermons on this parable, from the third century to the nineteenth. The tale, he says, is nearly always described as a rule of civil conduct, rather than an answer to the question, 'Who is my neighbour?' The answer to the question, for Illich, is not simply everyone, which becomes a meaningless platitude. 'My neighbour is who I choose,' he says, across the strangeness of differing tongues. Anyone who does this, says Illich, 'commits a kind of treason', and practises something 'utterly destructive to ordinary decency'.[13]

*

In times of numinous rupture, there will always be scores of migrants and wanderers who have become incomprehensible to their own, and found friendship in unexpected places of otherness. They appear as transgressive sorts, or as holy fools, swept up in the enigmatic comedy of the Spirit.

*

Pneuma is God as the gentle trickster figure. *Pneuma* is a mother who wanders through, opening windows as she goes; who welcomes strangers to the table, and the soup bowl never runs out; who tends the human ecology as a gardener who knows that biodiversity brings life. The *Pneuma* is the God who transgresses and breaks up all acts of enclosure, and the child who shakes up the snow globe.

*

We tend to build worlds against complex space. Complex space is a difficult thing to contrive or manage. It is, in part, an event, an interruption. Perhaps what we can do is position ourselves bravely toward the faultlines and be prayerfully open toward otherness. We can leave the door ajar on what we know and be curious about what we don't. My friend Vanessa Chamberlin once told me it's good to have one ear to the group and the other to the wall. In this respect, the complex space of messianic *ekklesia* requires an ingredient that it can't produce from its own parts; something over which it has no control. It relies on some other presence, that opens gates to strangeness one moment and divides in-group certainties the next. This is to say, complex space requires trust and a relinquishment of power.

Open *Ekklesia* Everywhere

I once encountered the Messiah on Showell Green Lane. Someone was in the throes of a severe breakdown. They stood in the road, covered in blood from self-harm, howling and cussing and pummelling cars with their fists. The traffic was in chaos and the whole neighbourhood came out. One group squared up to knock the person out. Others put their bodies in the way and took a beating to protect them. People who'd never met worked together. Others disputed. Everybody's shadow came out. Everybody was suddenly and meaningfully immersed in the shared questions of compassion, order and peace. Such is the messianic interruption.

The open gathering occurs in the tension between emergence and practice. On the one hand, it is a happening, similar to an unexpected arrival. On the other hand, there is an intentional practice of gathering and meeting across the lines. A life in the gathering calls for a kind of abiding attention to the spirit of what is occurring, a willingness to dance and to play the holy fool, and the bravery to be powerless and ignorant among people and situations we don't yet know about.

*

The open gathering reveals possibilities. These emerge when life experiences that are usually kept separate by the order of things slosh together on the tipping decks. We never learn more quickly than when we experience the powerlessness of otherness.

*

'We have been endowed with a *weak* messianic power,'[14] says Benjamin. And we also carry a messianic vision of the world as it might one day be, says Adorno.[15] In the open gathering, we open our hopes to complexity and revision. Our vision of the last things – of what a satisfying conclusion to our shared story might look like – becomes porous when we encounter one whose experiences have taught them to value different things. Our convictions about what ails the world also become open to revision when we encounter those whose different experiences

THE OPEN *EKKLESIA*

have placed them at odds with forms of power we had never much troubled over. The complex space of the open gathering is resisted as a menace. It's enclosed because its truth is found not so much in dogma as in encounter. The things we learn in the encounter are not so easily fixed down. Dogma and encounter need not be at odds if they carry the awareness that accommodates the other.

*

We may learn something about the practise of *ekklesia* from the protagonist of the Book of Ecclesiastes. The book takes its name after the character who narrates it. He is called, in Hebrew, *Qoheleth*, which means 'The Gatherer'. The discourse is meandering and bemused. It withdraws from all temptation to neatly synthesize and draw conclusions. *Qoheleth* goes about and gathers experiences: the things he has seen, done or read amid his encounters with others. These gathered images of life are placed alongside one another and simply allowed to be whatever they are. They're contemplated as a web of experiences in all their contradictions and complexities: a gallery of joys, injustices and unanswered questions. The only refrain that carries conclusive weight is that there is nothing better to do than to enjoy material life together, in food, love and good work. This is not so much the answer as, rather, the messianic question. All *Qoheleth's* gatherings are characterized by this practice of attending to real experiences, and refusing to control, categorize or dogmatize them.

*

The open gathering, as a common space of encounter, collaboration and reimagination, takes many forms. My friend Mike Love suggests the paradigm of friendship as the table around which we remake the world, one moment at a time. Friendship is a totally voluntary and non-hierarchical form of association. In friendship, reciprocity proceeds as improvised dance. Friendship is enspirited with joy and solidarity, and is not managed by law.

The voluntary association of different groups in moments of crisis and truth – for civil rights, for climate justice, against neocolonial wars, against developments that despoil and impoverish land for the profits of wealthy shareholders – these constitute spaces of open *ekklesia*, which appear and then disappear. These actions gather to challenge power and change policy, but all the while a slower and more mysterious change is also occurring. New relational connections are sparked. Resonance between people who might never have met creates new shared stories. The rewilding of Babel's mono-tongue is a yeasty ferment of encounter.

The complex spaces that emerge in moments of crisis also gather on the small roads, the local and the personal. Our addictions, struggles and personal dislocations gather us to find strength and resilience in spaces of open encounter. Alienated communities are thrown together by all that groans in the common spaces between enclosed homes. Emergency situations create solidarity, interdependence and reciprocity across lines of difference. Jazz has a way of transfiguring the clashing notes.

Open *ekklesia* emerges from the pursuit of a joyous common life. Our desire to break the lonely stranglehold of late capitalism fuels the voluntary creation of groups and associations who gather to think together, to sing and read poetry together, to share together, to walk, to run or to ride together, to trespass together. *Eros* forever struggles free of the boredom of enclosing independence toward mirth and reciprocity.

*

Since we've drawn out a distinction between the open *ekklesia* and the enclosing *kyriakon*, let's, even so, say a word in praise of temples. A *kyriakon* is certainly not the same thing as an *ekklesia*, but it is entirely possible that *ekklesia* might occur in a *kyriakon*, perhaps even on a regular basis. I have a love of temple spaces: the generous and open kind, as well as the strange and obscure; the storehouses of tradition, memory and awe; the sacred spaces that move in the dark, in a time deeper and slower than the froth of state and law. The first-century messianics met under a particular archway in their temple for as long as they could, before they were scattered by circumstance.[16]

THE OPEN *EKKLESIA*

The *Pneuma* and the open *ekklesia* may seem to be dangerous figures to the boundaried group, but only in the moment. In the long view, these rupturing disturbances might be their salvation, rescuing them from slow death by self-enclosure. They open windows to the anarchic breeze.

*

Origin stories often emerge in times of rupture and complexity. Some were called to wander from the land of their ancestors into a newness. Some began with the jarring novelty of love, a chance encounter between two parties by a well. Some began with tales of a figure who appeared to transgress the troubled orthodoxies of their own time, who embodied a striking new posture. But most complex spaces, if they don't blow away with the wind, tend to settle into a simpler and more enclosed form – hopefully a form that embodies what their originators believed was needful, good and lacking in the world. This is the way of things and I prefer to take it with good humour than to battle this accord with too much idealism, lest we turn our visions of complex space into a kind of ghastly law. Letting go is a good art.

Even so, even in that spirit, there is something Agamben once called 'destituent life'.[17] This would be a form of life that proceeds in joyous and organic coherence, while always resisting its becoming constituted as a wholly enclosed or legislated thing. It keeps an ongoing practice of relativizing itself, as my friend Paul Milbank puts it. Here is the beautiful mystery of a life that proceeds, always shifting a little to the side of law and hierarchy. The apostle Paul called it, with a wink of irony, *nomos pneuma zoen* – the law of the spirit of life – with *zoe* here meaning a creaturely subpolitical life, the kind we share with all living beings.

*

Someone once asked me what was particular about Jesus as a messianic figure. I've never felt Jesus was insecure. I've not felt the need to make enclosing claims of uniqueness on his behalf. I'm not sure whether the following is, in fact, unique, but I found myself gratefully observing that this figure whose greatness became immediately mythical was continually giving out tools with which to unmake whatever towers might be erected in his name. Within every saying there is a trap door that empties out all the power, leaving a fertile and generous *open*. Such is the strange art of unmaking ourselves as we go, in order to remain porous and open to *agape* and *eros*, and to the surprising gifts of numinous newness.

The Enclosure and the Open

Sometimes, to understand a thing, we may cautiously observe its opposite. My friend Paul Milbank and I had been looking for a word. We wanted a term to describe that precise moment when a grouping of people, or a movement or what have you, quietly and suddenly becomes set in its shared story, without consciously choosing to do so. It becomes haplessly boundaried in its membership. Its language and its imagination become self-referential. It is caught up in itself. This fascinating moment is fraught with hazards. Turnings and choices appear to pass by for the last time before the road is set. At this point, it will take an extraordinary flex of awareness to avoid slipping into chronic absurdity, irrelevance and self-righteousness. The bridges collapse almost wilfully. All the unknowns disappear and wisdom hardens into law and dogma. Things become cultish to the outside view. The group hums with confidence as it gathers its power inward, while appearing to be quite deaf to the world outside.

Paul suggested the language of 'objectivation', as described by the US sociologists Peter Berger and Thomas Luckmann, where a shared story begins to appear to be something that has always been so.[18] The world elsewhere becomes forgotten and strange. Whatever lies outside the walls is savage. Whatever lies outside the cult is damned. Whatever lies beyond the group's story seems uninteresting.

*

THE OPEN *EKKLESIA*

Moralizing against insular intolerance is boring and self-righteous. It always produces more insular intolerance. The mysterious moment of objectivation, however, is fascinating. It happens to all kinds of different movements, in different ways for different reasons. I think it happens to all of us. By thinking about these moments we can map the things that have been. We may even recover old choices we thought had long passed. The road might not be so straight or so objective. These moments are a liminal space, humming with anxious power and possibility.

*

I found myself returning to the language of 'enclosure' to describe this moment. There is, of course, the vulgar phrase in which they are said to be 'up their own arse'. They have become wholly enclosed in themselves, and intimately fascinated with the workings within while being absurdly unaware of everything outside. However, I was cautioned by my accordion player Mike Gilbert, that there ought to be a term that describes without judgement. He made the point that condescending language actively participates in the enclosure of the group, only from outside. We can't very well condemn what we join in with. Further still, if we pile in, enclosing others in their own worlds with dismissive language, we are at the same time enclosing ourselves in our own microverse, which prefers to rid itself of their complexity. Here is a road of mutual enclosures toward an atomized and alienated world. It's very difficult to abide with a vision that says that everything belongs.

*

Let's think about rituals. Once a grouping has become enclosed, its shared rituals will quite likely be understood as rituals of inclusion, by insiders and outsiders alike. The first-century *ekklesia* had two rituals that we know about: breaking bread and baptism. These are commonly understood as rituals of inclusion. To break bread, or take the Eucharist, is to belong to the Christian fold. To be baptized is the initiation ritual; a rite of religious conversion into the group. However, if we reach back to those stranger days when the *ekklesia* was a religiously diverse phenomenon, we might come to understand these rituals differently: not as rites of inclusion but as rites of *outering*. We could almost call them rites of exclusion.

*

Inclusion and enclosure are not quite the same thing, but they do sound curiously similar. Naturally, in a world beset with unjust exclusions from power, the language of inclusion has called aloud from the rooftops for justice. However, it's possible that this sort of imagination reveals an uncritical acceptance of those powers. It is only insisted that they should include more outsiders. And so we have to ask the question: inclusion into what? Industrialized development and progress? White privilege? Enlightenment? Religious truth? And what then remains excluded?

*

In the two rituals of the primitive messianic *ekklesia*, we find symbolic acts that speak precisely of exclusion and outering, not inclusion or enclosure. These are rituals of exit. They narrate the journey outward into an indeterminate open.

The ritual of baptism is rooted in the ancient story of the exodus. The Hebrew slaves were not struggling to be included more equitably in Pharaoh's power structure. They left it behind and wandered into the wilderness. The ritual of baptism was understood as a way of sharing in the political execution of a suffering Messiah figure. By being buried in the waters of death, one passed beyond the jurisdiction of the present powers who have enclosed the world in law. By rising from the waters, one was symbolically resurrected into a form of life beyond. Through baptism, one was released into an open, where the only law is love, or the spirit of *zoe*, of creaturely life itself.[19] Baptism was understood as a ritual of exit, from an enclosed and managed life under the powers of the present age.

The ritual of breaking bread was a meal of remembrance for the suffering Messiah who was executed outside the city. His was the kind of death reserved specifically for non-citizens. This was the ritual of the excluded. It is, I think, possible to *re-member* apart from the inclusion that implies enclosure. Re-membering involves the dismantling of enclosures that divide. The breaking of bread was a ritual of solidarity with the place of exclusion. It spoke of un-citizenship as the gateway to the open.

*

A while ago, someone told me a striking thing. He had previously been an ordained Baptist minister but had moved on to other kinds of work, and eventually was struck off the institution's list of accredited ministers for purely administrative reasons. He was thinking of marking this threshold of exit with a ritual of some sort. He found himself wondering about getting baptized.

*

Kester Brewin's book on piracy describes a somewhat parallel ritual to baptism in the raising of the Jolly Roger. Sailors, press-ganged against their will into manning ships for the British Empire, would occasionally gather, conspire and mutiny, taking over the ship from their masters. The skull and crossbones image, traditionally used to record the frequent deaths of sailors in the logbook, was reappropriated by the pirates. The trick was to bring the moment of death earlier into life, so that one might then at least enjoy freedom from the law of the living for a few years before one *actually* died.

The Jolly Roger was doubtless designed to inspire fear and supplication in the hearts of those they attacked, but there is something more profound and heartfelt in its symbolism. The skull and crossed bones [do] not just mean 'we are bringing you death;' rather [they announce] 'we are the dead.' We, the shat on, the abused, the flogged, the ones you treated as less than human, have escaped your power, have slipped away from the identity you foisted onto us. We, the ones you took for dead, are returning *as the dead* – and thus free of all fear, free of all human labels or classifications or ranks. We might say that the pirates did not raise the Jolly Roger as a symbol of violence, but rather as a declaration that no more violence could be done to them. They were dead, and yet lived still.[20]

THE MESSIANIC COMMONS

A short and crushing life as sailors in the service of a colonial empire was exchanged for a short but merry life as pirates. When they reckoned themselves dead, they were no longer subject to the harsh British rule that enclosed a third of the world. They lived on briefly as an anomaly, a blip of freedom, a passing glimpse of the open that waits after the end of all enclosing rule.

*

The US New Testament scholar Wayne Meeks called the breaking of bread 'the ritual of solidarity'.[21] To participate was to be in a web of solidarities. First was solidarity with the peasant Messiah who was brutalized, who met the death of the colonized, enslaved and criminalized. Second was solidarity with all suffering. There was a story told by this Messiah figure, before his execution, in which it was said that wherever a person might encounter the criminalized, destitute or impoverished, they had there encountered the Messiah in the form of that person.[22] When the gathered ate the bread and drank the wine, they did so in embodied solidarity with suffering and broken bodies everywhere. And so, third, it was a ritual of solidarity between the gathered themselves, who were religiously, ethnically and economically diverse.

Writings from the time tell us that the ritual became absurd when the wealthy ate the bread and drank themselves merry, while being served by the members of the community who were enslaved persons; or when the privileged men ate first and gave the leftovers to women and children at separate tables, as was customary in the Greco-Roman world. For this reason, the ritual was to occur with all together at the same table. There was no head seat. If there were, it would be for the oppressed and enslaved because theirs was the social location of the ever-migrating Messiah.

*

Breaking bread is a ritual of embodiment. It is absolutely material, and it re-members those who eat it to material life. It sits strangely between the mirth of food, company and sustenance, and the visceral brokenness of a body: blood, life, violence, vitality. It's tactile, and all the more so for its politicized mysticism, of the Messiah who shapeshifts, appearing in the form of one person and then another. It's about the politics of bodies. It chances the foolishness of messianic claims while also saying that one may never know in what form the Messiah might appear. We may walk alongside the Messiah for miles and not know it, even while talking with them about messianic things. We may pass the Messiah in the street, and miss them altogether, or commune with them and not know it.

*

To speak of rituals is partly to recognize the open *ekklesia* as something that is not devoid of content, meaning and story, for all its openness. The open *ekklesia*, in the messianic tradition, was centred on these things: on the messianic suffering of marginal bodies, and on the vision and practice of a world beyond enclosure. These rituals were not markers of religious sameness. Messianism is a kind of rupturing, and the drawnness of everything to everything against all acts of separation.

These energies have long been held in Jewish thought as two messianic figures. One is the Messiah ben Joseph, who is the suffering servant of the broken present. The other is the Messiah ben David who brings the peace of the messianic age. Between them is the groan; between the sufferings of the marginalized and excluded, and visions of an open, beyond inequity.

*

What then shall we say about this or that tradition? What of temples? What about the particular? What about distinctive stories, communities, tribes and groupings? Is there anything to be said of these? 'Much in every way,' as Paul would say again and again, since he was often accused of being too much the anarchist. These, he said, 'were entrusted with the oracles of God'.[23] Numinous ruptures and open gatherings do not exist to do away with such things but to hold them joyously aloft in the parade.

*

An *ekklesia* may indeed be any old gathering. This is a sketch of the open *ekklesia*; a rare and beautiful thing that relinquishes itself to befriend otherness and difference as it goes. But to reach further still, messianic *ekklesia* is something that lives in the groan between the realities of broken, embodied life and shared visions of hope. This *ekklesia* is a gathering of difference, around suffering life, toward life redeemed. The present calls for a culture of *Qoheleths*: gatherers who attend to and abide with what is occurring where difference meets.

Notes

1 Taubes, *Occidental Eschatology*, pp. 18–19.
2 Meeks, *The First Urban Christians*, p. 51.
3 Bonhoeffer, *Letters and Papers from Prison*, p. 92.
4 Theodoret, *Ecclesiastical History*, p. 32.
5 See James 2.2.
6 See Acts 11.12.
7 See Acts 9.43.
8 Acts 15.9.
9 See 2 Samuel 7.1–13.
10 'Divided tongues [*glossai*], as of fire, appeared among them, and rested on each of them. All of them were filled with the Holy Spirit [*Pneumatos*] and began to speak in other lanuages [*glossais*], as the Spirit gave them ability' (Acts 2.3–4).
11 See 1 Corinthians 14.
12 Cayley, *Rivers North of the Future*, p. 51.
13 Cayley, *Rivers*, pp. 50–1.
14 Benjamin, *Illuminations*, p. 246.
15 Adorno, *Minima Moralia*, p. 247.
16 Under Solomon's Portico, Acts 5.12.
17 Agamben, *What Is Destituent Power?*, trans. Stephanie Wakefield, https://icamiami-org.storage.googleapis.com/2017/06/17534719-agamben-what-is-a-destituent-power_-.pdf (accessed 20.8.2024).
18 Berger and Luckmann, *The Social Construction of Reality*, p. 78.
19 'For the law [*nomos*] of the Spirit [*Pneumatos*] of life [*zoes*] in Christ Jesus has set you free' (Rom. 8.2). There is further discussion of the Greek word *zoe* in the next chapter.
20 Brewin, *Mutiny!*, p. 53.
21 Meeks, *The First Urban Christians*, p. 157.
22 See Matthew 25.31–46.
23 Romans 3.1–2.

4

All Things

Of *Bios* and *Zoe*

Giorgio Agamben tells us that the Greeks had two different words to describe what we might call 'life'. One is *zoe*, 'the simple fact of living, common to all beings'. The other is *bios*, 'the form or way of living proper to an individual or a group'.[1] *Zoe* is raw, natural life. *Bios* describes the social, political, cultural life of humans, the particular structures and stories we build around ourselves.

These words didn't particularly strike me when I first read about them in the opening pages of Agamben's *Homo Sacer*. The distinction doesn't seem so complicated that it needs new (or old) words to illuminate it. But even so, something about the ongoing drama between these two words for 'life' has grown steadily in my mind. They come into relief in the haze after Modernity. Everywhere I go I find myself greeted by *zoe* here and *bios* there. I overhear their conversations and their dissonances. I find myself wandering through the complex spaces where they coexist, and the numbed spaces where they're held apart by dull violence.

*

These two words describe two very different things – not at all two versions of the same thing. They're not opposites of each other or two parts that make a whole. Nor are they inherently in contradiction, in tension or at war. They're not an either/or. But like all things that come to be and encounter each other, they have shared story. It is a contested story, as all stories are contested, but only *bios* contests it, and only to itself. *Zoe*, it is thought, contests nothing. *Zoe* just is.

*

We human creatures are absolutely both. Very *bios* and very *zoe*.

*

Agamben's telling of the story of *bios* and *zoe* is fraught in the extreme. He often refers to *zoe* by the bleak and vulnerable alias 'bare life'. I believe he picked up this language from Walter Benjamin's essay, *Critique of Violence*,[2] where it describes human life under the force of the state. And so, Agamben's political philosophy tells the story between *bios* and *zoe* something like this: our rights, our guarantees and dignities as human beings – our *bios* – are all in the safe-keeping of whichever political body we belong to. We have these rights and dignities because we are citizens of somewhere or other. If we are citizens of nowhere, as stateless people, as refugees, as 'illegals', as unregistered people or whatever the case may be, then we fall beneath the safe ground of *bios* and into the bleak and savage netherworld of *zoe* or *bare life*.

*

'If you believe you are a citizen of the world, you are a citizen of nowhere.' These were the words of then Prime Minister Theresa May at the Conservative Party conference of 2016. She was talking about immigration. Her rhetoric was aimed at those who felt equal solidarity with people outside the state. There's a warning in these words, or even a threat. It's a vivid telling of Agamben's story. The state, which is a made-up thing, a commonly shared act of the imagination, is a 'somewhere'. The material reality of the planet we live on is a 'nowhere'. So be careful where you pledge your allegiance, lest you stray to the lostness of bare life.

The state, on the other hand, is the safe-keeper of our *bios*, our common life as human beings. The state is a story told against *zoe* – against our creaturely life – which is envisaged as a sort of no-man's land. Anything outside citizenship is outer darkness.

There aren't words to describe the strangeness of this idea: this liturgy that ascribes concrete reality to a common fiction, while speaking of the material reality of shared creaturely life as a naive and immaterial fantasy. This is a linguistic trick of Modernity that remains normative, hidden everywhere in plain sight. Material *zoe* seems everywhere to be a subreality next to our cultural and political imaginations and inventions.

*

We should remember that a state, or any other political body, is not just the safe-keeper of *bios* but also a form of *bios* itself. Nor are political bodies and their outworking the only things we might call *bios*. Social conventions are *bios*. Art is *bios*. Religion is *bios*. Queueing, the rain dance and agriculture are all patterns of *bios*. Agamben's story is the story of a political philosopher describing the things that hold a decisive political power and the right of violence over our bare life as human creatures. And it is the *zoe* of human beings that concerns him in particular, more so than 'the natural world' in general (as we've come to call it). He describes, in the most disturbing terms, how our own *zoe* has been subjugated by our *bios*. We are divided within the site of our physical bodies, mind over matter, as it were. And so the story of *bios* and *zoe* has become a story of the colonizer and colonized.

*

When a refugee encampment formed in Calais in 2015, the French powers didn't hold back from ploughing through people's tents and makeshift dwellings with bulldozers. Meanwhile the British government quietly built a wall to keep those people from crossing the Channel to England. Nobody thought twice about calling that settlement 'the jungle'. The contempt for stateless human life and for nature itself were synonymous and astonishingly unhidden.

*

From the Greek word *zoe* we have, of course, the word 'zoo'. Here, *bios* understands *zoe* as a wonder and a spectacle to be domesticated, to be managed by bars and thick glass, as both a danger and an amusing curiosity. Just as museums become the trophy cabinets of colonial history, the history of the zoo might tell us something about the relationship of *bios* to *zoe*, in the spoils of colonized nature. Certainly, the term is synonymous with a realm of undesirable chaos, or uncivilized foolery. We should remember that Africans were being kept in European zoos until the 1950s.

Meanwhile, the animals that presume to live freely among us are called pests and vermin. We consider them unclean because they are willing to live amid the refuse that characterizes our dwellings. Much of the world has been arranged to exclude, remove, enclose or suppress *zoe*.[3]

*

I've heard it said that there will be a sure mark of the Anthropocene for the geologists of distant futures: a layer of rock in the earth's crust thick with numberless fossilized chicken bones.

*

Extractive capitalism is a very pure and aggressive form of *bios*. It understands *zoe* as sheer resource. Zoetic space is a realm from which materials are taken to be transformed by work into wealth for a realm of sheer *bios*. The waste products are then returned to the realm of *zoe*. Don't shit where you sleep, as they say. Gradually the process has created the illusion of a clean divide between the two realms. We seem almost thoughtlessly compelled by some sort of cleanliness anxiety to separate them out. This is partly because the compulsive psychosis of extractive capitalism requires the divide, in practical terms, and partly because systemic guilt requires losing all relational connection with the abused party. We mistake soil for dirt. We tar over it as though it were immodest.

*

ALL THINGS

And yet here we are: wholly *bios* and wholly *zoe*. The mockery, denial, suppression, colonization and exploitation of *zoe* constitute the repressed contempt in which we hold our own embodied lives. We divide and deny ourselves.[4]

*

Bios is so much more than these things. To be sure, this is only a part of the story; and it is *bios* itself that tells it, because how can we not tell this story now? We have to tell the story to subvert it and to unmake it or, at least, to make something different alongside it. *Bios* is unimaginably diverse, and yet here is that thing that we have to behold: the *bios* that has attempted to enclose the world.

'I put nature on the rack and torture her, until she gives up her secrets.' This quote is often erroneously attributed to Francis Bacon. In fact, it came from Gottfried Wilhelm Leibniz, the German philosopher, who was summarizing Bacon.[5] At the dawn of the scientific Enlightenment, Bacon did indeed use an alarming collection of metaphors to describe the newly discovered processes of experimentation: 'You have but to follow and hound nature in her wanderings, and you will be able when you like to lead and drive her to the same place again,' he said. 'Neither ought a man to make scruple of entering and penetrating into these holes, when inquisition of truth is his whole object.'[6] Bacon was a barrister of the royal court, a scholar of law. He used the language of trial and inquisition to describe the scientific method. The common feminine gendering of nature on trial and the masculine language for human inquiry sound a particular note at the turn of the seventeenth century. At that time, tens of thousands of women were being tortured in the witch trials, which sprang up wherever common land was being enclosed by private ownership and land-based people were being forced toward waged labour.

Here is Francis Bacon in a gentler mood: 'Nature to be commanded must be obeyed.'[7] This sounds less shocking, partly because most of us still regard nature as something wholly other to the human; something to be reckoned with and commanded. Man displaces himself from nature, from *zoe*, so that he can return to it as conqueror. He displaces his own *zoe* from himself and reimagines his own body as machinery.[8] The witch-hunts are, in part, the story of woman's refusal.

Francis Bacon is often quoted today, not because he is the cause of anything that wasn't happening anyway but because he had the clarity to describe the meeting of *bios* and *zoe* under the terms of progress; a clarity that was quickly lost in the enthusiasm for all kinds of discovery. Outrage at the language of the past means nothing if we can't see it alive and triumphant in the dominion of the extractive machinery into which we're now wired. The head plays with philosophy quotes while the body suffers.

*

Here is the story of *bios* and *zoe* once again. This time it is told by Standing Bear of the Oglala nation.

> I know of no species of plant, bird or animal that were exterminated until the coming of the white man. For some years after the buffalo disappeared there still remained huge herds of antelope, but the hunter's work was no sooner done in the destruction of the buffalo than his attention was attracted toward the deer ... The white man considered natural animal life just as he did the natural man life upon this continent, as 'pests.' Plants which the Indian found beneficial were also called 'pests.' There is no word in the Lakota vocabulary with the English meaning of this word ... [The Indian] was ... kin to all living things and he gave to all living creatures equal rights with himself. Everything of earth was loved and reverenced ... [To the white man] the worth and right to live were his, thus he heartlessly destroyed. Forests were mowed down, the buffalo exterminated, the beaver driven to extinction and his wonderfully constructed dams dynamited, allowing flood waters to wreak further havoc, and the very birds of the air silenced. Great grassy plains that sweetened the air have been upturned; springs, streams and lakes that lived no longer ago than my boyhood have dried, and a whole people harassed to degradation and death. The white man has come to be the symbol of extinction for all things natural to this continent.

Between him and the animal there is no rapport and they have learned to flee from his approach, for they cannot live on the same ground.[9]

It isn't conventional in my circles to speak of springs, streams and lakes as having 'lived'. Where I come from we say that expired batteries have 'died'.

The Tail Doesn't Wag the Dog

Here, then, are stories of *bios* and *zoe*. Francis Bacon announced the rule of *bios* over *zoe*. Agamben, at the far end of Modernity, called it out as the total power of the state over the bare life of the individual human. Standing Bear saw the genocidal and ecocidal march of whiteness against everything that lives. Today, the idea of self-inflicted human extinction has entered our imagination, even those of us who have inherited the dubious gains of this conquest. These are stories of a totally extraordinary historical epoch. And then there are other stories. If we consider the things from another sort of time, perhaps the sort that natural historians or geologists might swim in, then there are quite different things to say.

*

From deep time, it becomes immediately obvious that *bios* can't exist without *zoe*. *Zoe* doesn't need *bios* at all. *Zoe* existed for billions of years before *bios* emerged. They're not two of a kind; neither are they in any inherent contest. *Zoe* is a kind of miracle that emerged on a planet, and it remains mysterious and wonderful to us. *Bios* is another kind of miracle that emerged out of *zoe* and is, in fact, helplessly dependent upon it. *Bios* is the blink of an eye; the last half second of a long hot day.

*

When the language of human extinction wanders into the common imagination, most recently with the rise of Extinction

Rebellion and related popular movements, there is a sort of trauma to the imagination. I asked a Leeds University associate professor of theology, Stefan Skrimshire, about this. He said that we are presently experiencing the other bookend of the trauma that was felt with the discovery of deep time in the late eighteenth century, when geologists realized that the earth had been around for unfathomable periods of time before any human ever walked on it. Now we are sat with the strange thought of the earth carrying on as a living planet for unthinkable periods of time after humans have become extinct. This is not at all shocking to a modern-day geologist, but the religious sensibilities derived from the Abrahamic faiths have tended to imagine the final curtain falling on a world where the sound of human language, the drama of *bios*, is still onstage.

*

Suddenly the zoo seems presumptuous. What kind of mind envisages itself pacing around the torture rack on which he has bound nature itself? It's a Nero-esque madness. In deep time, *bios* is just a moment next to *zoe's* ocean-wide ages. It is a miraculous, beautiful, terrible and tragic moment.

*

'No music on a dead planet' has been the slogan of musicians involved in climate activism. Meanwhile, the artist Robert Montgomery's work tells a different story: 'When we are gone the trees will riot.'

*

The tail doesn't wag the dog, as they say. *Bios* comes from the life of the soil, and to soil it returns. The soil is more ancient by far, and the soil outlasts all human violence.

From the ground of Modernity, *zoe* is embattled and scraped out and enclosed behind glass. From deep time, human *bios* stands before *zoe* as a brief apocalyptic thing. It is small. It is fragile. It is glorious, foolish and brilliant, wonderful and incomparable. It has been said that angels pine over it[10] and that *zoe* groans for it.[11] It is so many different things all at once, and it is in need of some kind of redemption because it has, in part, put *itself* on the rack and doesn't know how to get off again.

*

There is a sense in which we only acknowledge the existence of a thing, with something akin to its full weight, when we are involuntarily confronted with its end. Art sometimes opens portals to this weight of meaning by creating spaces of apocalyptic experience. Religion does this too. It is no small thing to live in a moment when time and history reveal this stunning weight directly.

We nearly always tell these stories in a certain direction. We begin from where we stand. We start from historical time and think our way to deep time, from human to more-than-human. In this kind of storytelling, *bios* comes into relief; its strangeness and diversity, its beauty, magnificence, madness and smallness. We listen to the noise of its crises and the screeching of its wheels. Slowly a fine thread, hidden in plain sight, becomes perceivable to the relaxed eye. Its note finds the attentive ear. We cannot, now, say it too boldly. In storying its terrible dramas, *bios* looks toward long estranged *zoe* and says, 'I am not other than you. I am you. If I am not you, I am not anything. I put myself on the rack. I put myself behind thick glass. I despoil myself for profit, even for someone else's profit. How is the cavernous gap to be closed between us; between ourselves and our very *zoe*?'

*

In this space, I find myself able to feel two things, and they both surprise me.

One is this: if I can befriend again the displaced *zoe* of my embodied life-world, then the dreadful thought of our own extinction, which comes to us with odd seriousness these days, shifts and rests. I somehow think that I would remain a participant in the *zoe* that goes on afterwards. There is somehow enough. I take comfort in the latter days of rioting trees with their clapping hands. And who knows what wonders besides may occur? I learn to leave the greater space of hope for the things that I don't know.

The other is this: that I don't want *bios* to end, even if I did for a moment in my zealotry. Even in its deepest farce – especially in its farce – it suddenly seems beloved, pitiable and unaware of its own beauty. I want it to live. I want it to be for ever, somehow.

The Politics of *Zoe*

The drama of *zoe* and *bios* runs through religious stories in all directions. In some, we find the idea that *zoe* is of a lower, passing order because of its materiality. Where redemption is immaterial it becomes a thing of *bios*, a house built against profane *zoe*.

'Christianity conceives of redemption as an event in the spiritual and unseen realm, an event which is reflected in the soul, in the private world of each individual, which effects an inner transformation which need not correspond to anything outside,' says Gershom Scholem. Jewish messianism, on the other hand, 'always maintained a concept of redemption as an event which takes place publicly, on the stage of history and within the community'.[12] Here, redemption concerns *bios* on the ground of *zoe*, not removed from it.

Religion in Modernity has mostly been kept as a private and inward matter concerning spiritual things and other worlds, but not so much this one. Time and place are irrelevant. *Zoe* is irrelevant. For precisely this reason, there has been a slow and dull crisis of irrelevance for certain expressions of Christianity in return.

*

'I came that they may have life, and have it abundantly,' says John's messianic figure.[13] But what sort of life? That promise has been the vague selling point of all kinds for preachers looking for a following. We can hang on that word 'life' whichever meaning we like, whatever scratches the itch. The contemplative life, *bios theoretikos?* The life of pleasure, *bios apolaustikos?* The political life, *bios politikos?* In fact, John's Messiah says, 'I have come that they may have *zoe*, and have it abundantly.' Not the life of religion, orderly civilization or of inwardness (though not *not* those things either), but *zoe* – the creaturely life of the living planet, the life we share with animals and plants, and springs, streams and lakes. Natural life, we would say.

It's a strange statement. He speaks as though people didn't already have creaturely life. As though they found themselves somehow estranged from their own beating hearts and earthen bodies. Was *zoe* the thing people wanted? Was the statement somehow designed to suggest an unnamed lack? In what sense might people have felt alienated from the very *zoe* that animated them?

*

Zoe was synonymous with redemption among that first-century sect. Whether it be the mysterious mapping of 'the way, the truth and the *zoe*',[14] the mystical guidance of 'the law of the spirit of *zoe*',[15] the Messiah as the author of *zoe*,[16] or the tree of *zoe* as the end and purpose of the journey.[17] Hope is always the fullness of the embodied natural life of the soil. Hope is always held on the ecological plain.

The spiritualized turn of phrase 'eternal life' is the *zoe* of the *aeon*: the creaturely life of the age to come. This is the messianic liberation event that the natural creation groans toward:[18] liberation from the rack, from trees turned into public execution machinery and from 'those who destroy the earth'.[19] Across the New Testament texts, the liberation of people and natural life aren't just parallel or mutually dependant, they are described as the same event, very much in keeping with the tradition of the Hebrew Bible. The gentle shall inherit the earth and riot with the clapping trees and the shouting stones, while those who destroy the earth dig their own graves.[20]

*

What about *bios*? When the farmer cast seeds and some fell here and some fell there, it is told, in that well-known parable, that some fell amid tangling thorns and briars. There, they sprouted at first but were quickly overwhelmed and choked by the cares, riches and pleasures of *bios*, and so their fruit didn't mature.[21] It was after he had frittered away his *bios* in lust and gluttony that the prodigal returned from bleakness to be found once again by his father, 'alive' (*zoe*).[22]

Bios is also the drama of economic life and the choices therein. Amid the great shows of economic privilege, the impoverished widow is named as greatest because she gives the last of her *bios*.[23] Here, a person's *bios* becomes the resonance of God's love when it is passed to the needs of another.

Bios is also a way: a pattern of living, which is a thing to be crafted, cared for and attuned to wisdom; a thing to be lovingly fashioned. It is a realm of possibility, for good or ill. There is a sublime and awesome beauty to *zoe*; and there is another kind of sublime beauty to *bios*. The beauty of *zoe* is in keeping with its peaceful and immoveable sense of itself; it is at peace even in its rage. The beauty of *bios* lies in the drama of its fragility; its continuously undecided and unbearably consequential path. Angels long to look into these things.

*

Bios is a uniquely human kind of life. It casts itself in its own web of stories, structures and meanings. *Zoe*, on the other hand, would ordinarily be understood as an unstoried realm. However, in the messianic tradition, the bare life of creation is not wholly without a sense of story. Paul describes a prayer practice that breaks this distinction down. It is said that *zoe* longs and groans in resonance with the *Pneuma* toward liberation from the rack. And it is said human creaturely life, too, can join in with this prayer of *zoe*, which is continuously ringing through the creation. Crucially, this sort of prayer is wordless because this is a sacred space where *bios* must surrender to *zoe*, perhaps as the mind must quieten itself to rediscover its place in the body. They called this kind of prayer *systenazei*, which is commonly translated as 'groaning'.[24] In return, it was believed that *zoe* prayed (and prays) for the liberation of *bios*, for 'the revealing of the children of God'.[25]

Agamben says that, for the Greeks, it would have been absurd to speak of a *zoe politike*.[26] Political life is the exclusive province of *bios*. *Zoe* has no will and no political orientation. But there is a sense, in these messianic texts, that when the child *bios* is quietened within its greater holding in *zoe*, then *zoe* becomes, in a mystical way, a political space, as *bios* becomes a natural one.

All Things Reconciled

I spent a day with my friend the forager Miles Irving a while back. We ate a stew he cooked over the fire, of wild foods we'd picked in the woods. The flavours amazed me – earthy, floral, peppery – as familiar as the land I've always walked on but strange to eat. The stew was heady and herby and seemed somehow dangerous. It made me think of eating Korean food for the first time, of experiencing a completely new set of flavours and thinking, 'Well, this is what Korean food tastes like.' Here I was, eating food native to the place where I've always lived, experiencing flavours that were strange and familiar at the same time. I felt as if I were meeting someone I'd always lived with for the first time. There is a particular kind of bond with what we raise to our lips; a knowing, deeper than the intellect.

*

I've had a number of conversations with Miles about the stories that begin the book of Genesis. He has a striking interpretation. The humans in the paradise garden were, as far as the tale goes, hunter-gatherers. They didn't farm, they picked what the plants gave. Only with their loss of innocence and their coming of age did they enter the toilsome world of agriculture. They lost a relationship of trust with *zoe* and instead entered a relationship of controlling force over nature, from which they had distinguished themselves by way of the plough.

There are plenty of tellings of ancient history that will speak of the birth of civilization around the Mediterranean basin. This story begins with the new agricultural humans. It was this shift that gave rise to city-states and empires, walls and armies. The scientists Simon Lewis and Mark Maslin consider the agricultural revolution an early contender for the beginning of the Anthropocene.[27] The agricultural revolution made hierarchies necessary and gave rise to the religious structures that were used to justify those hierarchies.

I conversed again with Miles a little later. I had thoughts that had grown out of his thoughts and I wanted to see what he would make of them. These days, many people are looking through the Bible in the hope of finding the beautiful and balanced nature religion that they sense is needed. But the Bible is awkwardly unobliging. It is as full of cities, regrets, wars and political intrigue as ever. It seemed to me that the Bible is what it is because it emerged from the agricultural civilizations around the Mediterranean basin, with all their war, law, wealth and poverty. It tells stories about one exodus after another, from city states and empires, from slavery and from political corruption. These are texts looking for ways out of the structures that enthrone *bios* as the fallen and unhappy tyrant over *zoe*. These are texts of *metanoia*.[28] These stories long for the paradise of *zoe* because they find themselves painfully beset and homesick for the rest of creation, as I once heard Rowan Williams say.[29]

Miles met this vision with his usual curiosity and nuance. He saw a few more threads of zoetic wisdom in the Bible than my sketch of *bios*-angst gave credit for, and I was pleased to make more room for that.

*

Stories are complex creatures. The story above isn't intended simply to say that *bios* is farming and farming is of the devil. A look at how we farm will tell us a lot. The circumstances in Judea and Galilee in the first century show a *bios* that had become violently divisive. Jewish people were being taxed hard by the Romans. They were priced off the land that fed them and then obliged to work the same land as hired labour for colonial elites. They were caught in a totally fragmented situation; they had to sell their own bare life as labour to pay rent for land to labour on, to sell the food they farmed to pay taxes to the colonizers who had stolen the land. All this *bios* before they could even sit down and eat what grew out of the soil or swam in the sea. They were alienated from their own zoetic being by so many degrees.[30] Did they want *zoe* in its fullness in a *bios* of politically engineered precarity? Yes, I think they did.

*

Wherever *zoe* becomes private property, the tail wags the dog.

*

The US theologian Walter Wink tells a story that begins with the domestication of the horse.[31] Once people found they could tame horses, ride them and rig them to carry loads, it was suddenly possible for the people of one settlement to attack the people of another and carry off the goods. Once the *zoe* of the horse became enthralled to *bios*, settlements were obliged to adopt a defensive posture in the world. Walls, armies and taxation abounded. This tradition is unbroken to the present. No wonder the Psalmist feels uneasy around horses. McLuhan suggests that the invention of the stirrup, which enabled a person in heavy armour to mount a horse, created the whole political economy of late medieval society. He says that 1066 never would have happened but for the stirrup.[32]

*

In one story after another, we find ourselves in a maze of separations and alienations, all piling up in a chaos of order. Our *bios* removed itself from our *zoe* so that it could return as discoverer and conqueror. And one tier of *bios* is segregated from the next, in one controlling hierarchy over and across another.

Timothy Morton's advice to the person who would become 'ecological' is simply to look at oneself from a greater distance. We are part of the ecological whole. We cannot be otherwise. Here is a trick of perspective and perception by which we see past the tangle of divisions and separations. We are a part of all things. We're not an extra ingredient or foreign arrival.

*

Modernity tends to dissect things into multitudes of subjects and categories that needn't touch one another. For this reason, Modernity has great difficulty thinking about anything in the context of everything. Whether in religious theologies or in economic diagrams, Modernity is characterized by a goal-oriented tunnel-vision that considers everything peripheral to its pursuit as an unconnected irrelevance. Today, we are reeling with the sense that anything must be encountered in the context of everything.

Messianism is ecological. The Greek words *pan ta*, meaning 'all things', run through the messianic texts of the New Testament. All things are handed over by the old masters at the messianic event. All things are renewed.[33] All things are the subject of divine compassion and love.[34] The Messiah is a part of all things, and fills and permeates all things.[35] Time gathers toward the gathering of all things in the messianic event.[36] All things are reconciled,[37] so that God will be all in all.[38] If one part suffers, the whole suffers. If one part is missing, the whole is incomplete. The liberation of anything is tied up with the liberation of everything. These weren't innovations; the writers weren't pronouncing a new vision, not in this respect anyway. They stood in the long messianic tradition of Hebrew prophets that imagined the whole earth, all its peoples and all its creatures, saturated in redemption.[39]

This story collapses immediately when the Messiah becomes the property of a group who wish to further their own interests. Wherever this happens, redemption is elsewhere and that Messiah becomes an anti-Messiah: a colonizing, homogenizing *bios* all over again. This is not because the Messiah is a ghost with no identity, but because the Messiah is a fully autonomous other who can't be enlisted, used, domesticated or owned. That peculiar sect in the first century knew this, and they resisted all attempts to claim religious ownership of the Messiah. As they saw it, the Messiah could never be grasped by means of religious conversion.

*

While Modernity became a terrifying iteration of the *bios* that divides and rules, messianism is the future call toward re-integration, all things reconciled, the eschatological convergence, the scattered interspersing of measureless difference.

*

All things reconciled is the almost unthinkable thing: the redemption of *bios* by its reconciliation to *zoe*. All liberating and arighting work is the reconciliation of *bios* to *zoe*. It is the healing of displacement and division by the recovery of a relationship good enough to trust: no more the rack. Redemption is, as Williams describes it, 'the natural process of becoming natural'.[40]

*

The first-century messianics ascribed to *zoe* something the Greeks did not. The natural creation was capable of longing and purpose, since it was believed that the *Pneuma* animated it, and that it was drenched in *sofia*: God's wisdom.

The Greeks also denied that *zoe* could be a political space, since politics would be an expression of *bios*. The messianics thought otherwise. In the wordless groaning of *zoe*, they heard the cry of the soil that keeps the blood of the abused and oppressed against systems of subjection and death. To participate in that wordless zoetic groan of longing was to kneel prayerfully in zoetic political space, which sits outside the enclosing systems in which *bios* has imprisoned itself. Nature as political space doesn't sound as strange today as it once did. Here, amid flesh, leaf, soil and stone, amid the materiality of all things, is the ground on which to seek reconciliation. Here are the messianic commons.

Notes

1 Agamben, *Homo Sacer*, p. 1.
2 Benjamin, *Reflections*, pp. 277–300.
3 In a podcast conversation, Dr Rowan Williams described this to me in stark political terms: 'When we think of the bad old days in

South Africa, and all these signs saying "whites only", occasionally, I think there's just a little bit of an analogy with the world in which we're putting up notices saying "humans only", as if we really did not want to share our space with the rest of organic life.' Tim Nash and David Benjamin Blower, 'Everybody Now: Climate Emergency and Sacred Duty', *Nomad* [podcast], 16 February 2021, https://www.nomadpodcast.co.uk/climate-emergency-and-sacred-duty/ (accessed 21.8.2024).

4 'The effect', continues Rowan Williams, 'is of course to cut into our own flesh, almost literally' (Nash and Blower, 'Everybody Now').

5 I'm indebted here to the essay by Carolyn Merchant, '"The Violence of Impediments": Francis Bacon and the Origins of Experimentation', http://www.journals.uchicago.edu/t-and-c (accessed 20.8.2024).

6 Grey, *Sacred Longings*, p. 15.
7 Merchant, 'Violence of Impediments', p. 737.
8 Federici, *Caliban and the Witch*, p. 158.
9 Miller, *From the Heart*, p. 255.
10 See 1 Peter 1.12.
11 See Romans 8.19–23.
12 Scholem, *The Messianic Idea in Judaism*, p. 1.
13 John 10.10.
14 See John 14.6.
15 See Romans 8.2.
16 See Acts 3.15.
17 See Revelation 22.14.
18 See Romans 8.18–26.
19 Revelation 11.18.

20 Jesus' saying that 'the gentle shall inherit the earth' is a quote from Psalm 37. His ecological messianic image of the shouting stones resonates with the singing mountains and the trees clapping their hands in the Book of Isaiah, in which the redemption of creaturely life, human and more than-human, is a continual theme.

21 See Luke 8.4–15.
22 See Luke 15.11–32.
23 See Mark 12.41–44.
24 *Systenazei* means, crucially, 'to groan with'. That's to say, it's something done with another, with the *Pneuma*, or with the rest of creation.
25 See Romans 8.18–26.
26 Agamben, *Homo Sacer*, p. 1.
27 Lewis and Maslin, *The Human Planet*, pp. 113–46.
28 This is the Greek word commonly translated as 'repentance'. It means, literally, to think over or to rethink.
29 Nash and Blower, 'Everybody Now'.
30 The US novelist and poet Wendell Berry describes farming today in similarly fragmented terms in his essay, *What I stand For Is What I Stand On*. See pp. 23–35.

31 Wink, *The Powers That Be*, p. 40.
32 McLuhan, *War and Peace in the Global Village*, pp. 26–33.
33 See Revelation 21.5.
34 See 1 Corinthians 13.7.
35 See Ephesians 4.10.
36 See Ephesians 1.10.
37 See Colossians 1.20.
38 See 1 Corinthians 15.28.
39 See Isaiah 11.1–9.
40 Williams, *Looking East in Winter*, p. 19.

5

Sacred Spaces

Norm and Otherness

The language of sacredness and holiness calls with a gentle religious hum. Relic laden purity. The heady and smokey hall. Darkness and light. It's serious and austere. It is presided over, perhaps, by a fragile hierarchical authority that clings to disappearing archaic ground; or by a gentle order who carry mysteries, with quiet smiles. It is a place of odd peacefulness, where time seems to stand still. At its most settled and generous, it preserves a strange beauty, stored up in traditions that are offered to the world. Elsewhere it's fearful, threatened by deviance, in a losing stand-off with time. These are places, more than spaces; or, at least, spaces maintained in fixed places: a church or a temple or a place of mythic or religious significance.

*

The Hebrew word for sacredness is *kadosh*, from the root *kodesh*, meaning 'apartness': it is a kind of specialness, removed from the normal manner of things.

The Greek word translated 'holy' in early Christian texts is *hagios*, meaning 'different', 'other' or 'unlike'. So 'sacred space' might mean something such as *spaces of otherness*, where the normal order of things is suspended. In a sacred space, different possibilities and imaginations are entertained as guests. Or we become the guests of those other possibilities and imaginations. In the aura of this otherness, the present world may be experienced apart from the forces that hold it in its present *nomos*, its normal form or order of things.[1] In sacred space, the present

SACRED SPACES

world may be experienced apart from its prevailing systems and the domination of the present powers.

*

See those two Greek words next to each other: *nomos* and *hagios*, the norm and otherness, law and sacredness. Sacredness is a space of exception from law. Sacredness is the antithesis of *nomos*, as otherness is the antithesis of the norm.

*

A religious space might be an old caretaker to this aura of strange otherness; rooted in another time, an outpost of the past lodged in the present. This kind of time-folding space fosters all kinds of happenings, good and not good; but it is the wandering out of normal space into some kind of elsewhere that is of note here. On the other hand, a religious space might not be a sacred space at all. It might not hold a quality of otherness or make any discernible break with the *nomos* of the world and its powers. It might, in fact, uphold the present order. All the while, the world is full of irreligious spaces of otherness. Acts of civil disobedience, therapy, temporary autonomous zones, political strikes, spontaneous play, art spaces, campfires, dramatic performances, acts of kindness, honest conversations and the shedding of tears, to name just a few.

*

The New Testament story hangs on the proposal of a messianic figure, who comes and gives a blink-and-you-miss-it glimpse of everything made new. Then he goes, leaving everything as tragic and broken as ever it was, with enigmatic promises of a future return. Here is a strange Messiah who reveals hope and then immediately hides it again.

Giorgio Agamben's thoughts on this always lead him back to ideas about 'messianic time'. The person who accepts the messianic proposal above, by an inward flex, lives across two times at once. They live in the present age in all its tragedy, wonder, violence, power, loss and deathliness, because when else can they live? But they also live in the coming age of wholeness, peace, balance, reciprocity, wisdom and, above all else, love; though they don't yet find themselves in that time. They live *in* one age, and *of* the other, as the saying goes. They live now, as citizens of an age that has not yet begun. They fancy that, if they live it now, then of course it *has* begun in embryonic form, as a seed in the dirt of the present.

*

Messianic time is a powerful idea, but try to live it. To live in the broken present as a citizen of a healed and all-embracing future will turn life into a continual path of perplexing choices, subversions and transgressions. It is a beautiful pattern to live by. It's mad, costly and potent, lived tentatively across glimpses.

The messianic story above opens the possibility of transforming our realities by shifting our allegiances from the dull rule of the now to a visionary space of possibilities. To imagine the world healed and whole, and then to live in the light of that untethered vision, is something we do every day in small ways. The more bravely and purposefully we do it, the further it leads us into the kind of commitments that will cost us.

*

All this is to speak of messianic time. These notes are not so much about time as about space. What might messianic space be? Where are the messianic spaces?

Messianism is held in a vision of two times: the present age and the age to come; the way things are today and the way things might be if they were healed and made whole. To speak of messianic space is to speak of real physical spaces in the present tragic age, where the life of the age to come might emerge, even briefly. Messianic spaces are spaces of exception in which the powers that enclose the world in systems of domination, violence, control and tragedy are suspended. A bubble appears, if only for a short time, holding those powers outside of itself. It forces out a space where life exists, momentarily free of domination and management. Allegiance to the law of the present momentarily drops.

SACRED SPACES

In this kind of space we are relieved, for a time, of the coercive demands that ordinarily weigh on our bodies, our nerves and our imaginations. What might emerge within us if we were to live more and more of our lives in these kinds of spaces? What might emerge between us if we were to live together in and out of these spaces?

*

Would we unleash untold violence and chaos? Would we call a state of exception from the law, envisage a brave new world and then impose it by force? Why would a space of otherness, free from the restraint of law, not result in idealist tyranny toward a new perceived certainty?

Walter Benjamin described two kinds of violence (and then a third, but that's not for this discussion).[2] One is the violence that sustains law, such as policing. The other he calls establishing violence; an event that creates a new law, such as a conquest or violent revolution. Both kinds of violence exist in the service of law. Both kinds exist because of a hubris of certainty.

But the age to come is an unknown. It's obscure, mysterious and uncertain. Who can guarantee it? Who can prove that it exists? Who can show us around and explain it all? All knowing is partial. All seeing is through mirrors, dimly. Ask any good messianic figure about the age to come and you will get enigmatic stories about farming, fishing, weddings, wars and buried treasure. Even those who share the same religious traditions diverge wildly in their future myths and eschatologies. All pre-boxed visions of the mystery are false. They're not the age to come. They are a seamless continuation of the present age, with its power struggles over truth and its scramble for certainty. Messianic space exists in tension between the now and the not-yet, between what is known and what is unknown. 'I'm not predicting the future,' said McLuhan, 'I'm trying to predict the present.' Messianic space becomes impossible wherever the age to come is being packaged and sold by anyone. The people in this business want power. They're setting up a new law. Their business belongs to the present age.

Sacred space doesn't make its own pronouncements about

the future, but suspends the prevailing noise of the present, making space for whatever numinous thing will emerge of its own accord.

*

In this sense, sacred space is a kind of prayer that is practised by hosting, subverting or attending to a space. It is a kind of abiding somewhere, quietly sweeping aside the prevailing *nomos* to create a sort of emptiness in which something might occur, a space of numinous possibility. It may be that such a prayer is answered, and something of the age to come takes root in the present and begins to enlarge and awaken like a little yeast in the dough: a space of otherness, a space apart, an unlike space. It is this I'm wanting to call sacred space.

Of World and Earth

In the year King Uzziah dies, the prophet Isaiah is in the temple, or at least he dreams that he is.[3] He sees winged serpents in flight,[4] and they're chanting: 'Other! Other! Other!' They sing on: 'The earth is full of God's glory.'

Here is a liturgy of otherness and earth. I recall that my friend Dougald Hine noted a resonance between this chant of the dragons and the prayer that Jesus teaches: 'Other be your name ... your kingdom come ... on earth as it is in heaven.'[5] There's a glitching together of different worlds in this apocalyptic scene, of strangeness and here-ness all at once. The vision is a frightening and dreamlike glory, alien to everyday experience, which nevertheless calls itself an earthly thing; a reality that belongs here, hidden in everyday experience.

*

Sacred space is characterized by a sort of dislodging feeling. We're untethered by its spell from the grind of the real world. We're released to float for a time into a realm of vision. We fall into the spaciousness of our immaterial gut. Perhaps it feels a little like leaving the weary bones of embodied life and going to another realm, where we find what we need in order to return and continue.

Or, we can flip it. When we enter sacred space, we pass out of a world characterized by immaterial abstraction and disembodiment. We pass out of a world that is mostly fashioned of made-up things. We land deeply and viscerally in our bodies, in our material reality. We enter a space where embodied truth is untethered from its abstract world-binding.

*

In recent years, Christian theology has revelled in the dramatic language of 'in-breaking'. The kingdom of heaven is breaking into the world, presumably from outside. However, the apocalyptic language of the New Testament works consistently in the opposite direction: in the direction of out-breaking. The kingdom of heaven is not coming from somewhere else. It is within. It is among. It's is being revealed, liberated from its binding, uncovered or found from where it has been bound, buried, occupied and suppressed. Sacred space doesn't call to a gnostic mystery over yonder but to what is already present, hidden in plain sight.

*

The Greek word often translated 'world' in the New Testament is *kosmos*, which means, literally, 'system'. This might refer to naturally occurring systems but, more commonly, it refers to human-made systems, orders and structures; the way we build the world around ourselves, between our desires for stability and power. The Greek word for earth is *gês*, which means, literally, the soil, the material substance of the planet we live on.

Similarly, the Germanic etymology for 'world' is *ware-auld*, meaning 'human-age'. This is something conceptual: a human era. Earth, on the other hand, is the material stuff we live on and are made of. Worlds end all the time. New worlds begin quite often, as the mountains see it. Worlds are passing things. Earth is a slower and more constant realm. Worlds are made up of all kinds of material and immaterial things, such as ideas, stories, roads, phone boxes, bank balances, titles, amphitheatres, temples, vows, passions and paperwork. Earth is an irreducible material reality that holds a multitude of worlds.

*

This doesn't mean that the world is profane, and that sacred space is of the earth. Sacred space is, rather, a messianic vision of world and earth reconciled. Sacred space interrupts the world only because the world suffers from the compulsion to break its life-giving relation to the earth; to saw off the branch it sits on. The world believes it manages the earth, just as *bios* believes it can keep *zoe* in a zoo. In the fever of this normative madness, a sacred space is a space of reconciling to what is, to material reality. It is a space of substance in a world that spins yarns.

*

Faerie is a sacred space. 'Fantasy is made out of the Primary World,' said J. R. R. Tolkien on the relationship between the enchanted realms of otherness and material life. 'It was in fairy-stories that I first divined the potency of the words, and the wonder of the things, such as stone and wood and iron; tree and grass; house and fire; bread and wine.'[6]

For Tolkien, the escapist dimension of faerie stories is not a fanciful retreat but a mode of liberation. 'Why should a man be scorned, if, finding himself in prison, he tries to get out and go home? Or if, when he cannot do so, he thinks and talks about other topics than jailers and prison walls?'[7]

*

Enlightenment Modernity has reached its point of despair and self-betrayal. It sprang from the European intellectual revolution that understood itself to have overcome superstitious beliefs with a scientific view of material reality. It wanted to jettison primitive fancies in favour of hard facts. But the bent of this process led toward all kinds of disembodying abstractions. It abstracted humans from nature, so we could colonize it as though we were discoverers from elsewhere. It abstracted humans from their own bodies by favouring the intellect over the body and separating the two. This way we could colonize

SACRED SPACES

one with the other, subjecting the body to experiment, improvement, servitude, slavery and horrifying selectivity; so that we could use our own bodies as economic resources or as fodder. Today, the world is full of camps, which are full of forcibly detained human bodies.

*

Modernity was inclined toward separating things out for the purposes of categorization, use and control. The etymology of 'empire' leads us to the language of ordering and systematizing and categorizing. Empirical knowledge was the stuff of Modernity, and Modernity was the intellectual climax of empire.

*

Nomos is about drawing lines that are not to be crossed. It places boundaries and borders between things. It is the disintegration of things, for their own good and in the interest of stability; or it is for the good of those who make the law, in the interest of control and power. Modernity was the incremental imposition of an empirical intellectual *nomos*, which gradually separated everything out from everything.

*

The irony of enlightened and sober Modernity is seen in the power of its imaginative creations, which are ubiquitous to its world. Nation states and borders are imaginary things. European exceptionalism and white supremacy are imaginary things. Money and wealth in the capitalist *kosmos* are imaginary things.

The economist Kate Raworth's redrawing of Samuelson's economic circular flow diagram is a good example.[8] In Samuelson's image, money flows in a loop from businesses to households and from households to businesses. Households take the money through wage labour and give it back by going to buy what businesses produce. But what is this fiscal abstraction that flows around the loop? What does it have to do with material goods? Where do material goods actually come from? Where do they go after use? Where does power lie, and what does it arc towards?

Samuelson's diagram is totally enclosed and abstracted from the whole. Raworth's proposal, to redraw economics in the image of a doughnut, is about the endlessly complicated task of re-integrating economics into the whole *oikos*.[9] It is about re-integrating the abstract concept of wealth back into material reality, planetary limits, natural cycles and human ecologies. It is about reconciling all things. The controlling bent toward dis-integration leads straight to judgement day.

*

While Modernity pushes anything other from itself into the realm of fantasy and fancy, we who live under its dull *nomos* are perplexed to find ourselves oddly removed from material life, from nature and from our own bodies. We are obliged to occupy ourselves continuously with the abstractions that Modernity has cast on the world.

Sacred spaces, as spaces in resonance with another age, are those where we might encounter something real, truthful and material. They are spaces of momentary return to all things, back to the beautiful and dreadful realities of the whole, of which we are part. They're spaces where law, which separates us out from living participation with everything, is suspended. In the safe holding of a well-held sacred space, we may chance that fearful encounter. We might survive it and be changed by it.

These are spaces of personal renewal and re-integration. And they are political spaces of rebirth, from the present order of things into the alternative patterns of another time.

*

'There are no sacred and unsacred spaces; there are only sacred spaces and desecrated spaces.'[10] The intentional practice of sacred space is the practice of repairing the world. It's the practice of making space amid desecrations, for the revealing of things as they are, in their wholeness and their holiness.

*

SACRED SPACES

Every therapist knows that an encounter with things as they really are is likely to be painful, frightening, surreal and costly.

*

'Sacredness' and 'holiness' are used more or less interchangeably for the Greek *hagios* and the Hebrew *kadosh*. The etymology of holiness leads us to the language of wholeness. It's fitting, from a messianic perspective, that concepts of otherness and wholeness come together. The messianic imagination reaches for wholeness in the shape of all things reconciled, but the pain of the present age is of separation, dis-integration and abstraction. Sacred spaces are spaces of reconciliation to what is.

*

When Isaiah finds himself in sacred space amid chanting serpents before God, he's afraid. Everything shakes and smokes. He is jolted out of the froth of his day-to-day *nomos* into an experience of deep otherness. And then he's sent back to his world with this dispiriting message:

> 'Keep listening, but do not comprehend;
> keep looking, but do not understand ...
> Until cities lie waste
>   without inhabitant ...
> like a terebinth or an oak
>   whose stump remains standing
>   when it is felled.'
> The holy seed is its stump.[11]

The Oglala Lakota Russell Means speaks similarly:

> All European tradition, Marxism included, has conspired to defy the natural order of things. Mother Earth has been abused. The powers have been abused, and this cannot go on forever. No theory can alter that simple fact. Mother earth will retaliate, the whole environment will retaliate, and the abusers will be eliminated. Things come full circle, back to

where they started. That's revolution. And that's the prophesy of my people, the Hopi people, and of other correct peoples.[12]

Spaces of Exception

Messianic time is exciting because it's elusive. The state polices space but it can't police time. It occupies a landmass marked out by imaginary boundaries and presides as absolute law over it. But it's trapped in its own time. Somewhere in our deepest innards, we're able to find ourselves free of the state's rule, by declaring ourselves citizens of another time: a time when the state is no more.

*

To speak from the messianic tradition, we should note that the age to come is full of tribes and cities. On the other hand, there are no states in the age to come, nor any empires for that matter. The state and the empire both pass away in the end because of their common original sin: they both impose law upon land. They're both an occupation. They both separate themselves out from what is, in order to return to it as conquerors. The age to come is the coming end of all occupations. The age to come is the fullness of nativity and indigeneity: all things reconciled.

*

Roald Dahl's *Fantastic Mr Fox* lives amid human settlements. He is a feral animal, free of all law. He is held and guided by a community of relationships good enough to trust. In Wes Anderson's film, he rides down a road on a motorcycle with his son and his nephew. They stop when they see something in the mountains: a wolf on a snowy ridge. Fox raises his fist in a sign of solidarity. The wolf raises hers in return. Indigeneity and the feral life of the city resonate together. They both resist occupation.

*

But while messianic time is exciting, it's also rather insubstantial. Theology and political philosophy have said much about messianic time in recent years. So much talk under the bedsheets with a torch: it's exciting, but what does it do? When does it happen? Where does it happen?

If we can imagine messianic time and affiliate ourselves with it (and why not? We imagine borders, finance and royalty easily enough; we fight wars over these fictions), if we can pledge allegiance to messianic time, we can surely imagine messianic space. Indeed, we can imagine it, image it and incarnate it. Messianic space is nothing but the incarnation of messianic time, however fleeting, in the present. It is the embryo of the age to come in the womb of today. Messianic space is messianic time, manifest now in space and matter.

*

To hold a sacred space is to hold a space of exception. The Jewish intellectual Walter Benjamin and the Nazi political theologian Carl Schmitt made a common observation. In Schmitt's words, 'he is sovereign who calls the state of exception'.[13] This is to say that when a head of state declares an emergency and then then gives themselves licence to make and break laws as they see fit, they place themselves beyond the law. This person is the author of the fictions we all live in. Benjamin concludes that, really, all state law comes into being this way, and we live forever under this state of emergency, or this state of exception. The state itself *is* a state of exception – a special measure imposed on us for our own good.

So, Benjamin says, our task is to call our own state of exception within and against the state's state of exception.[14] A double negative: we are displaced from a displacement; exiled from exile; abstracted from an abstraction. From the state's perspective, it's a fantasy; an attempt to live on no ground. From the field beyond, it is an escape from the fantasy of the state and a return to the soil itself.

The stakes today couldn't be higher. We now find ourselves obliged to throw off the yoke of the state's economy of law, power and endless parasitical growth because the state is throwing off all creatureliness. A sacred space is political. It's a space of exception from the state's state of exception.

Now, see the comedy go back and forth. Extinction Rebellion's foundational document declares that our contract with the state is broken, and so rebellion is our sacred duty. The state has responded by creating new laws to make it more difficult for people to break their existing laws. They create a state of exception to prevent people from calling their own state of exception to the state's original state of exception from nature.

*

Messianic time is certainly exciting, but messianic space is actually dangerous. To practise messianic space is to practise an alternative political body, and possibly to put ourselves at odds with the powers that be. It's one thing to speak enigmatically about a space that suspends law but, at some point, we might even find ourselves straightforwardly breaking it.

*

Here's another scene. A small gathering of Wet'suwet'en tribal members stand blocking a road in so-called British Columbia. They call down the road to the Royal Canadian Mounted Police: 'This is Chief Woo's land. You are not welcome.'

The state wants access to the forest because it's made deals with logging companies to have the trees cut down and turned into lumber. It wants access to the land because it's made deals with oil companies to pipe crude oil through it. The Wet'suwet'en want to protect the ancient forest on land that was their home long before the state we call Canada existed.

The state of Canada claims rights over the resources within its borders and enforces those claims by violence. The Wet'suwet'en were rounded up at gunpoint, arrested and detained. They continue non-violently to uphold their way, which precedes the state's law and is rooted in relationships good enough to trust.[15]

What is revealed in this clash between the lore of old relationships and the law of young states? They who hold the monopoly on violence make and wield the law because it is they who can

SACRED SPACES

threaten and enforce consequences. An alternative political creature is formed apart from the law, apart from violence. It speaks with another kind of authority, from enclaves of messianic otherness. It is formed in sacred spaces.

*

At its best, law carries noble aspirations. It's an attempt to preserve the world against chaos in an age where relationships are not good enough for us to live in fluid improvisation. We can't free ourselves of law faster than we can build good relationships. Neither is the state the only source of world-enclosing law, nor the only political structure to speak of. *Nomos* rests on us in many forms, though all are connected. This sketch serves to show that sacred space is political, and messianism is a question of citizenship.

Practising Sacred Space

I once heard someone talk about the time she would spend in the cathedral near to where she lived. 'It's not paradise,' she said, 'but you can see paradise out the window.' What was it about that environment that made it, to her, a liminal space between the sufferings of the present brokenness and a dim image of the age to come, through the glass, darkly? How do such places come about and who keeps them?

*

John the Baptist is the first and only child of Zechariah and Elizabeth. He would be expected to continue his father's priestly work in the temple, since they are Levites by tribe. But John chooses not to.

Perhaps it seems to John that the temple is not functioning as a sacred space. It is absorbed in the rule of the present. It is in the keeping of the Sadducee party, whose policy is to make deals with the European occupiers, to keep their world ticking over as smoothly as they can. It resists messianic folklore. It resists the life of the age to come. It keeps an uneasy truce with the injustices of the present.

So John takes his sacred work to the wilderness. He goes down by the riverside. He hosts a space where the hierarchical *nomos* of the Sadducees' temple order is parried. He hosts a space where the violent *nomos* of the Pax Romana is kept outside. He finds a little ground.

Here, he hosts and performs rituals of submersion and emergence. People take turns to submerge their bodies under the surface of the cool, moving water. They bury themselves in a symbol of death to the present order of things, and then they emerge as participants in the life of the age to come – the hazy myth of all things made new. This is an exodus. They break their vows to the powers of the present age and emerge as citizens of another.

This is a space of *metanoia*, a thinking over: a rising above the broken law of now in order to rethink it, to think past it, to think differently.[16] This is a space of *exomologou*, a space of, literally, 'speaking out together'.[17] As a collective act, they open their mouths and speak the buried truths that the present *nomos* represses, the conceits and oppressions that are silenced. Truth is welcomed as a dangerous guest, as a powerful stranger. This is a sacred space.

*

Sacred spaces, as we sketch them here, always involve two things.

One is a physical space where the prevailing laws and norms of the present are somehow suspended. This might look like all sorts of things, from purposeful acts of civil disobedience to simply 'forgetting ourselves' for a moment and behaving outside the expected norms, or experiencing the world on a plain other than the one served up to us each morning.

The second is an empty chair at the table, so to speak. The empty chair is a space for the emergence of what cannot and should not be planned or managed. Truth, as an autonomous other, is welcomed as a strange and dangerous guest who guides toward possibilities of healed futures and toward the hazy dawn of the age to come. In this respect all sacred spaces are acts of prayer. They 'leave space for X quantities' as the US artist and musician John Cage puts it.[18] They invite the real to emerge, however it wishes, without controlling outcomes. They are spaces of possibility where something may or may not happen; and whatever might happen, no one can say with certainty.

*

Therapeutic practice might be a sacred space. Here, one person may speak out to another things they can't ordinarily say. Norms of social law and inner policing are temporarily suspended, and so secrets may be revealed. Welcoming the guest of truth will be disturbing, fascinating, frightening and many other things, but the outering of what is normally tethered in world-binding is the necessary event for life transformed.

*

Civil disobedience is a sacred space, where the law is openly broken in order to disturb the normal running of things. By exposing the faultline between law and life, between power and experience, between *bios* and *zoe*, truth is free to emerge. Where does power lie? What is its nature? Who or what does it serve? What does it want? Where does it flex? Where does it break? Where does it double down? At what cost does it relent? Civil disobedience is a revealer. It breaks up power and opens possibilities.

*

The carnival of public protest is a sacred space. The normal aura of the street is suspended. It is flooded, instead, with an *ekklesia* of people awoken to a spectacle of otherness. The sound and vision of hidden rituals, suppressed cultures, tribal energies and folk religion emerge toward life transformed.

*

The Jesus Prayer of the Orthodox tradition runs, 'Lord Jesus Christ, Son of God, have mercy on me, a sinner.' Those who pray this practise sacred space in their bodies insofar as the

Jesus they invoke is a messianic figure beyond all law, who is invited to come and calm or suspend their own regulatory *nomos*, to reveal hidden truths toward healed futures.

*

An artwork always alters space. Art transforms ordinary space into sacred space when it interrupts the one-way street of the now by introducing a disturbance or, perhaps, by producing an immersive experience of otherness.

'The artist sets a trap,' says McLuhan. Their work trips us out of ordinary time into otherness. He adds, 'The artist builds models, or Noah's arks for facing the change that is at hand.'[19] They create temporary spaces that hold the violence of a degenerating present age aside for a time. Something opens.

The visual, aural or tactile work is an invitation to be stilled, to be in one's body and to be met by whatever emerges. The law of imperial time is suspended and truth is allowed to emerge. The common unwillingness of artists to explain that their work is what it is in order to preserve it for the task of messianic space. The truth that emerges must do so in its own autonomy.

*

In their mournful, Dante-esque garb and with deathly white faces, the Red Rebel Brigade hold sacred space as they walk through the streets.[20] Their silence breaks the spell of business as usual. Their visual otherness breaks the facade of the grind. Their sorrowful poise breaks the forced ethic of *keep calm and carry on*. They speak out together in wordless loss.

*

Sacred spaces emerge as subversive occupations. If the state can be seen as an occupation of land by law, subversive occupations of space within the state are a sort of double negative: temporal bubbles of messianic piracy.

In order to protect their ancestral land, the Wet'suwet'en have built small houses in the path of the oil company that is attempting to run pipelines through it. Dwelling on the land and refusing to obey eviction notices suspends the law of business and state. It reveals the truth: the ongoing grind of colonial history. The revealing of these truths opens the possibility of other outcomes.

*

The giving of gifts is a practice of sacred space, suspending the divisive rule of economic competition and enclosure. It invites truth to emerge in a space of trust, reciprocity and gratuity. Gift economies, skill-shares, useful unemployment, pay it forward schemes and the like are practices of messianic space in which alternative economies may emerge on the basis of relationships good enough to trust.

*

We could go on to speak of hospitality, hosting and guesting, of rituals, of kindness, of silence, of daring the unaskable question, of openness to chance encounters and more. There are all kinds of modes through which we may practise this; all kinds of patterns that interrupt the iron law of the present and pull out a chair for the powerful stranger of truth.

How to make a safe space for a person to fall apart? Where shall we go to fall apart ourselves? How does the trickster, the jester or the holy fool break the spell of normality? When is it wise and fitting to reach for the wire-cutters? When is it worth getting arrested? Where are the cracks through which the light gets in and when shall we go there? How does a wall collapse before the simplicity of kindness, thoughtfulness or empathetic perception?

John the Baptist has a practice. He holds messianic space. He thinks through where, how, by what rituals and which modes of participation. He does it because messianic spaces are ways of finding paths into possible futures. This is an elusive art to be learned and passed on. May there be sacred spaces everywhere.

The modes and particulars are always different. They can't be mapped. This is about improvisation. But underneath run *pistis*, *elpis* and *agape*, an attentive posture of loving faithfulness to all things and the dangerous glint of hope that calls us to mischief.

Notes

1 In the New Testament, the Greek word commonly translated as 'law' is *nomos*.
2 Benjamin, *Reflections*, pp. 284–9.
3 See Isaiah 6.
4 The word 'seraph' means 'serpent'.
5 Matthew 6.9–10, my translation.
6 Tolkien, *Tree and Leaf*, p. 60.
7 Tolkien, *Tree and Leaf*, p. 61.
8 Raworth, *Doughnut Economics*, pp. 16–30. Paul Samuelson (1915–2009) was a US economist.
9 *Oikos* is the Greek word for 'home', from which we derive words such as 'ecology' and 'economy'.
10 From the poem 'How to Be a Poet' by Wendell Berry, https://www.poetryfoundation.org/poetrymagazine/poems/41087/how-to-be-a-poet (accessed 22.10.2024).
11 Isaiah 6.9, 11, 13.
12 From a speech given by Means in 1980. See Russell Means, 'Revolution and American Indians: "Marxism is as Alien to My Culture as Capitalism", *Films for Action*, 12 November 2011, https://www.filmsforaction.org/news/revolution-and-american-indians-marxism-is-as-alien-to-my-culture-as-capitalism (accessed 20.8.2024).
13 Agamben, *State of Exception*, p. 1.
14 'The tradition of the oppressed teaches us that the "state of emergency" in which we live is not the exception but the rule. We must attain to a conception of history that is in keeping with this insight. Then we shall clearly realize that it is our task to bring about a real state of emergency' (Benjamin, *Illuminations*, p. 248).
15 For more information on this struggle, see https://www.yintahaccess.com.
16 *Metanoia* is the Greek word commonly translated as 'repentance' in the New Testament. It literally means to think or know (*gnosis*) over (*meta*).
17 *Exomologou* is the Greek word commonly translated as 'confession'. It means not so much private introspection as a collective speaking out of the truth.
18 From Sister Corita Kent, 'Immaculate Heart College Art Department Rules', https://designmanifestos.org/sister-corita-kent-immaculate-heart-college-art-department-rules (accessed 2.10.2024).
19 McLuhan, *Understanding Media*, p. 71.
20 The Red Rebel Brigade is a performance art troupe that has been appearing at environmental demonstrations since 2019.

6

Transfiguring Work

Nobody Creates Wealth

The following reflections grew out of a symposium on the theme of craft. Things often begin with a feeling around for definitions, and so an initial definition of craft was suggested. I can't remember it well enough to do the sentence justice, but it involved mastering skills in order to create goods. I felt some misgivings in myself around the language of creating goods, value or, worst of all, wealth. I became quite pedantic about it. Why was I so insistent? There is, among religious folk, a defensive anxiety that says 'only God creates', but it wasn't from that lofty place, I don't think. The disquiet came, rather, from the dystopian landfills of late capitalism and its optimistic language of wealth creation. Those that capitalism applauds as 'wealth creators' are really just moving things around that already exist until there is a lot of money at their own end and a pile of rubbish at the other, where the wretched of the earth are consigned to scavenging. It is oddly fantastical to believe that anyone creates wealth or anything else. There is no wealth apart from what already is, apart from what is native to the biosphere. Those called 'wealth creators' are mostly just moving things from extraction to manufacture to the dump; they are subjecting creation to futility.[1] I trust the language of wealth creation like a parent who asks, 'Where did you get that?' and hears, 'I found it.'

These are questions of economic justice; but, more specifically, I was thinking of the harm done to our sense of being in the world, our sense of being human creatures. It was to do with the crafter's relationship to what they craft and, then, by extension, to all things (of which they themselves are part). It seems to me to be an ugly trap of a Modernity world view, to regard the miracle in which we find ourselves as mere stuff that is worthless when we find it and only becomes a *good* when we act upon it. Or worse still, it's viewed as the raw fuel by which we generate wealth. This sort of imagination alienates us from everything. I suspect it alienates us from ourselves. I think we would want to craft ourselves out of this anthropocentric, extractive and self-alienating vision. As John Ruskin, the nineteenth-century art and social critic, said, 'There is no wealth but life.'[2]

*

Even many wooden chairs are not a greater good than a tree. But good chairs, perhaps around a good table, open up possibilities and pleasures. They release things worth releasing, if well judged. Songs around a wood fire are not a greater good than all the good that an old chair has carried over its many years, but this too releases a dormant value in the old wood and in the scene that surrounds it when the time is right. The crafting of furniture cultivates a relationship of love and respect for the inherent good of the tree, which industry might easily become alienated from.

*

The theologian Hannah Malcolm's book *Words for a Dying World* collects reflections on climate grief from different places in the world. I noticed that accounts from the Global South were generally characterized by a crisis of shared identity between land, creatures and communities; meanwhile, accounts from the Global North were characterized by feelings of personal guilt, sadness and a sort of loneliness. I asked her why she thought that was. She replied, 'Extractive capitalism is lonely.'

*

Where I'm from, the banknotes all have on them the words: 'I promise to pay the bearer on demand the sum of X.' If I take the banknote to a bank, what will they give me in return? I suppose, long ago, they might have taken the note and given me gold, but money isn't tethered to gold anymore. Now they take the note – which is not really money but a token for money, which is itself essentially a token – and they will make an alteration to the cauldron of numerical abstractions kept mysteriously behind the counter by their strange arts, and I will come out ten pounds richer and with nothing in my hands.

What if I go into a shop with the ten pound note – which is not really ten pounds but only a token representing ten pounds (which is a real thing that no one has ever seen) – and I offer the note to the keeper with its strange inscription: 'I promise to pay the bearer on demand the sum of ten pounds'? Will I walk out with ten pounds? No, I will walk out with a few second-hand books. The shop will not have ten pounds either, but only a note that demands they are paid ten pounds. The wizard is always behind another curtain.

Money is a fascinating abstraction; it's stranger than black holes. In any case, it's important to our broader constellation of thoughts to note that money used to be a sort of system of tokens that kept tabs on the passing round of goods. The goods were what mattered. Money was just a way of passing IOUs. But at some point, things flipped and goods became a means to the end of amassing money. Capital became the prime good, even though no one has ever seen it; even though, like borders and sovereignty, it is a shared act of imagination.

*

I would like to know if this switch might coincide with the language of wealth creation, which comes to us from Modernity, with Adam Smith's descriptions of a transformed economic world. Did anyone believe they were *creating* wealth in medieval times? They were creating grandeur and power perhaps; but wealth was amassed through avarice, not created. Most of the world lived by subsistence and trade. Did ordinary people believe they created their food and shelter when they grew turnips and constructed homes from natural materials? No, they cultivated what already was. But when the world changed and ordinary people worked for bosses who paid wages, wealth became a product of *bios* rather than a quality of *zoe*. Ever since then, most of us have been swept up into the collective work of conjuring.

*

The language of avarice – the sin of amassing wealth – was left behind in the medieval age because in Modernity it was no longer thought a sin. According to the German sociologist Max Weber, it might have been understood as a mark of one's assured salvation or righteousness.[3] Tony Stark (Iron Man of the Marvel franchise) embodies the common belief that salvation comes from the hand of those who have successfully amassed wealth.

*

Wealth, collected up into the sheer abstraction of untethered money, is that astonishingly pure thing: *bios* in its raw form, entirely refined of all traces of *zoe*.

Zoe suffers under the abomination of raw *bios*. *Zoe* is butchered and discarded to 'create' this formless subject of religious reverence, this immaterial fetish, this uncarnate stuff. In this respect, wealth creation, from material life to abstract wealth, appears to be a kind of diabolical process of disincarnating everything.

*

Homo economicus is the name given by classical economics to the human being understood as a creature governed by fundamental self-interest. Beneath this miserable tier is another one: the creature governed by want for sheer fetishized abstraction and for raw, abstract power because of its hold over the collective imagination.

*

Here are two steps of alienation.

The first is to see something only as a good, or as wealth, once it has been formed into something of use. Before it is acted on, the material world appears neutral, inanimate: a closed space, with no intrinsic meaning or good. This way we are alienated from everything and anything that we have not yet exploited.

The second is that we see the things we have made not as

wealth but as part of the means of wealth creation. The wealth itself is the nothingness of money for which we exchange the things we've made. In this way, we inevitably find ourselves making jaw-dropping volumes of all kinds of useless and unbeautiful things that end up discarded in the sea and the soil. We don't create wealth; on the contrary, we have become a machine that turns the wealth of creation into uncompostable waste in order to generate a sheer abstraction for a handful of celebrated wealth creators.

*

Today, you can buy a small plastic cast of a stick and pretend to be Harry Potter, with a wand. All the while, real sticks unnumbered lie neglected in the woods because they lack the aura of authenticity that comes from plastic and a monetary transaction.

*

For years, we've been finding animals strangled to death by plastic waste and whales washed up with guts full of rubbish. Now we're finding microplastics in the bloodstream of human foetuses. It is fascinating that none of this awareness has caused significant change.

*

Here is a map covered in contour lines of alienation. The generating of wealth by producing meaningless goods is achieved by hierarchies of power, so that some use the labour of others as part of the process by which they generate abstract wealth for themselves. We're alienated from our own ability to work, selling our labour as a thing separate from us, to those who use it to further works of alienation.

If the messianic *telos* is the reconciliation of all things, we might amuse ourselves here with some dramatic religious pronouncements.[4] We might call our economic order an anti-Christ. Here is an all but unstoppable machine that works against the reconciliation of all things. In fact, it works hammer and tongs toward separating everything out from everything. Good is abstracted from nature. Wealth is abstracted from good. Work is abstracted from the human person. One group of humans is abstracted from another. All humans are abstracted from nature. It's a series of boundaries; a complex of concentric rings that enables inner circles to exploit outer spaces by degree and type.

This is a characteristic of Enlightenment Modernity with its love of empirical knowledge; it is compelled to sort, order and categorize everything into separate units that can be understood, used, mastered, controlled or owned. Modern economics thinks likewise. In the present flood of interconnected crises and possibilities, the tools of Modernity look ridiculous. Modernity has very little in its box of tricks that might help to reconnect everything it has separated. We're all looking for the back door.

*

To remedy these concentric rings of toilsome alienation about our work, the nineteenth-century designer and social activist William Morris suggested two things: first, collapse the class hierarchies that enslave the work of one group to the wealth creation of another; second, stop making anything that is not, on balance, good, useful or beautiful.[5] If wealth creation is no longer the goal for which a powerful group is commandeering the work of others, there is no longer any reason to fill the world with disposable, fetishized rubbish. The unnatural division between goods and wealth collapses. The unnatural division between work and human purpose collapses. And, importantly for Morris, if everyone does some work and there are no wealthy slackers in glass towers, we wouldn't need to make nearly so much and we could all have a little more blessed rest.

But beneath these social and political changes there is a more elemental question. How do we re-situate ourselves and our work as part of the whole thing? With the Enlightenment human civilization began to look as though it were an alien invasion, colonizing nature as something other and then working to extract its resources. How to recover a sense of absolute belonging and mutuality with all things?

*

TRANSFIGURING WORK

Most of what we call 'history' has been held within a twelve-thousand-year epoch of stable climate that geologists call the Holocene, a Garden of Eden in the story of the biosphere. Today, the argument is made that we have entered a new, far less stable geological epoch called the Anthropocene, triggered by the human activity of wealth creation in the Modern era. If the proposal to recognize a new geological epoch is accepted, then the Holocene will be demoted from an 'epoch' to a 'stage', or perhaps wiped off the record completely, since it has been so anomalously short. Professors Simon Lewis and Mark Maslin have suggested 1610 CE as the start of the Anthropocene.[6] This date marks the beginning of a massive dip in atmospheric carbon dioxide caused by European colonization of the Americas and the forming of a single global economy of the 'wealth creation' kind.[7] How then shall we now be still and be stunned by the awareness that our intellectual, spiritual and economic bent toward the dis-integration of all things has run so far, to the depths and heights of the heavens and the earth? How odd, at the end of an age of disenchantment, to see science itself reeling and re-enchanted with a kind of grief-awe, reaching to open doors beyond itself.

*

These sketches explore the tipping point when money went from being a thin system of tokens, which represented goods, to being the wealth itself, thus creating an unprecedented appetite for worthless goods. It went from being a system of tokens for things to becoming the main event.

Moralizing about greed and economic injustice seems like pointless noise these days. Power is deaf, or it joins in the moralizing clamour itself, to oddly numbing effect. All kinds of people are absolving themselves with empty words and gestures, as though the issue were merely quantitative. A little to the side of all that noise, there are people standing and watching the strange way that we are grinding through a protracted and miserable judgement day that continuously degenerates because our economic imagination moves steadfastly toward the dis-integration of all things. They're abiding in transformative grief-stricken awareness of this astonishing spectacle: as we dismantle nature, we dismantle ourselves because we are nature. As we dismantle creation, we dismantle ourselves because we are creatures among creatures. We are the creation that we dismantle.

The Ends of Work

We're walking a path someone else laid for us, and they say there is no other path. How to escape this story of un-creaturing? How shall we reimagine the works of our hands? What retelling of the tale might ground us in work that re-integrates us and reconciles us? How might we re-form work within relationships good enough to trust?

To ask the question in a messianic tenor: what is work in a world made whole? The present age is dis-integrated and alienated from itself, and must be held together by law against chaos and violence. As an act of love toward our descendants, let's imagine an age to come when all things are released from this subjugation. Let's imagine, even if it's an imperfect fantasy, life in unmanaged equilibrium: all things re-integrated and reconciled in creatureliness. We are beginning to play with a different *telos* of work: not making new things but making all things as new, in good and healed relationship.

I go to my friend Mike Winter with questions on all matters biological. He told me that Darwin didn't advocate for the survival of the fittest but for survival of the *fit*; that is, the survival of the fitting.

I find myself drawn to the language of transfiguration. There is a story in which the Messiah is transformed, but not into someone or something different. It would be truer to say that the transfiguring was a revealing of the Messiah's hidden, dormant *isness*.[8] In a messianic theology, all things move toward their transfiguration, toward being released into and revealed in their deepest being and wholeness. They move 'collectively deeper into what is real', as the theology scholar Annie Dimond put it during our craft symposium, perhaps not into settled states so much as good relations.

*

In the Greek language of 'life', the *telos* of Modernity is the conquest of *zoe* by *bios*. But *zoe* is before *bios*, and will outlast it. *Zoe* doesn't need *bios*. *Bios* is wholly dependent on *zoe*. Redemption depends on the reconciling of *bios* to *zoe*. This task is the messianic *telos* of craft and of all work.

'I have come that you might have *zoe*,' as the messianic saying goes, 'and have it in fulness.'[9]

*

A *telos* is a hazardous thing. When our *telos* becomes overly fixed, we get stuck on the one final outcome as we've envisaged it. We become tyrannical in bringing it about. Who are we to say with certainty what something is, in its transfigured form? Lived experience tells us that the road goes on and work is never complete. We're creatures. And so it was that Annie Dimond suggested the word 'translation' alongside 'transfiguration'. While craft might be understood in a wide frame of redemption, the word 'translation' loosens things: it was not quite wrong; I have not made it quite right; it will not stay as I have translated it; but it will be translated again and again, as will I myself.

On the other hand, translation suggests remaking the form of a thing rather than revealing it, as transfiguration might suggest. Messianic work is a kind of savvy dance between these two words. One always involves an ingredient of the other. Good work finds wise balance and virtue in our creaturely participation in something much bigger than we are and that is always somewhat hidden from us.

*

The language of translation and transfiguration goes across the work and the worker. It envelops both. Everything is translated. Everything is transfigured. The seed translates the soil to a vegetable. The animal or person translates the vegetable to nutrition and life energy, which finds its way back to the soil and grows something else. It is not a 'lesser' that is translated by a 'greater'. Everything is translated. Even the Messiah.

*

In her essay *Learning the Grammar of Animacy*, Robin Wall Kimmerer writes about the process of learning her native language, Potawatomi. At the time of writing, there were only nine fluent speakers left. She describes her difficulty in following the grammar of a language in which, unlike English, there are so many more verbs than nouns. She recounts reading through the Potawatomi dictionary: '"to be a hill", "to be red", "to be a long sandy stretch of beach", and then my finger rested on *wiikwegamaa:* "to be a bay". "Ridiculous!"'[10] But in the end, she finds that this re-verbing of the world restores a sense of its animacy, its aliveness and autonomy:

> A bay is a noun only if water is *dead*. When *bay* is a noun, it is defined by humans, trapped between its shores and contained by the word. But the verb *wiikwegamaa* – to *be* a bay – releases the bay from bondage and lets it live. 'To be a bay' holds the wonder that, for this moment, the living water has decided to shelter itself between these shores, conversing with cedar roots and a flock of baby mergansers. Because it could do otherwise – become a stream, an ocean or a waterfall, and there are verbs for that, too. To be a hill, to be a sandy beach, to be a Saturday, all are possible verbs in a world where everything is alive. Water, land, and even a day, the language a mirror for seeing the animacy of the world, the life that pulses through all things.[11]

*

My friend Sam Ewell often tells a tale: his friend Claudio looks him sternly in the eye while holding aloft a banana peel, saying: 'Do not call rubbish what God has called good.' Then he throws the peel into a tub of worms who eat it and break it down into fertile compost. There is no such thing as waste or rubbish in an economy of translations.

*

TRANSFIGURING WORK

The *telos* of things is not to be transformed into what they are not by the will of those who prefer them that way. This is what Paul calls 'creation ... subjected to futility'.[12] The telos of everything is to be what it really is, in its web of relations and translations. All deviations from this truth create roads of dissonance, each to be resolved in one judgement day or another.

*

Kate Raworth's explorations into the iconography of economics are instructive. She compares a diagram used to illustrate economic growth with a series of traditional images.[13] The first is a line that ascends at an angle, forever onward and upward in its hapless march. The others are circular and made of weaving images and arcing movements: a Celtic knot, a yin-yang symbol; their lines also go on endlessly but within a spacial limit. They do an endless dance; not only endless, in fact, but also without beginning.

Raworth's doughnut image is somewhere between the two. It shows a finite space with inner and outer limits. Growth goes on until it can go no further at the outer limit of planetary resources. Growth may recede but not fall below the inner limits of poverty and deprivation.

If we approach Raworth's image as if we were classical economists inhabiting the story of wealth creation, then there are only two directions to go: outwards and inwards. The limits are a kind of *nomos* that we have to observe because if we go past them, all kinds of chaos will be set loose. But if we learn to recognize the limits, not as a law but simply as an encounter with what is, then something wonderful happens. Our disappointment is turned to joy when we learn to dance. We end the immature, linear, backward and forward motion of Sisyphean Modernity, of wealth creation, which can only understand categories of more and less. The space in which we can live becomes transfigured by an improvised weave, with no beginning or end. This joy only emerges from loving awareness for the scope of what *is*, from a relationship of care and attention. It comes of abiding.

In the myth of wealth creation, the meaning of work is quantitative and transactional. In the myth of transfiguration, the meaning of work is qualitative and reciprocal. It is the practice of improvising within a web of relationships good enough to trust. Classical economics traumatizes the whole by breaking the bounds with its linear lack of imagination. And then it withers by itself in outer darkness.

*

In the familiar, old Protestant language, salvation is by faith, not works, *pistis* not *ergon*. Paul's endless back and forth with these terms was aimed at dismantling all quantitative and transactional routes to the age to come. Those ways always appeal because we can guarantee them by our own hand, but in the end it remains the case that we can't take paradise by force, or else it is paradise no more. The Jewish Torah knows this. 'Love is the summation of the Torah,' says Paulos.[14] Meanwhile, the cassette tapes of Reformed preachers using the language of *faith* versus *works* to exhort people towards a transactional work of becoming a Christian as the cost of avoiding hell, these would stack to a thousand miles high and play for a thousand years.

Our work means nothing, says Paulos, if not rooted in faithfulness, if not rooted in relationships good enough to trust.[15] And the appearance of such relationships are a lie, says James, if not played out in transfiguring work.[16] The present system, says John, is overcome not by might nor by power but by relationships good enough to trust.[17]

*

'Our particularity is our window on to universality.'[18] Work in the global village occurs in the village. Work that occurs in the nebulous global cloud of capital addresses the village in general but not in particular. The relationship is not good enough to trust because there is no relationship. Transfiguring work is mostly small and present and embodied. The global commons are formed by localities; common work in service of life.

Incremental Exodus

There is a common thread between the paths of John the Baptist, Jesus and the fishermen disciples. They all chose to withdraw themselves and their labour and skill from economies and powers that, they judged, were not in the service of life.

Jesus was a builder.[19] Ched Myers suggests that he would have been enlisted with other local labourers to work on Herod's grandiose building projects near Nazareth, obliged to spend his days sustaining himself and his family by building monuments to that puppet ruler of the Roman imperial power. Herod was not building relationships good enough to trust. He was building a presence too intimidating to disobey. His operation existed outside any relationship of trust.

John the Baptist should have followed his father's path and become a priest, offering prayers and incense in the temple. But the temple was now ruled by the Sadducee party who were shoring up their power by making deals with the Roman occupiers. Theirs was the reliable crookedness of 'realists'.

The disciples worked in a food economy that was being enclosed and taxed by the Roman powers. Jewish people were working as hired labourers on land and seas they had never ceded. Everything they grew and caught made their colonizers richer and more powerful.

Jesus, John the Baptist and the disciples quit their jobs. They continued with the work they had done before, but they turned it toward the service of life. The fishermen became fishers of men (as Myers puts it, they set nets and hooks for corrupt powers). The son of the temple priest opted out of that centralizing institution to host gatherings on the margins instead; radical subversive rituals for ordinary people. The builder quit building palaces for kings and instead began building a folk *ekklesia*. It is with some poetic justice that they actually ended up being sustained by money that was leaking out of Herod's household via Joanna, the wife of Herod's steward, among other radical women who believed in redistribution.[20] That said, the move was extraordinarily reckless for poverty-stricken Jewish people under a brutal occupation. Perhaps they only did so because

THE MESSIANIC COMMONS

they sensed (correctly) that they were close to a total social and political collapse anyway, and so they threw caution to the wind.

All this begs the questions: what kinds of social, political and economic powers co-opt work in the service of death, and how then can work be liberated from them? When and how does one quit?

*

Here's a different story, more savvy than reckless.

The imperial beast as a machine of extractive wealth creation haunts the New Testament from one end to the other. It begins with Caesar registering his occupied colonies for taxation.[21] Tax collectors awkwardly wander the pages as traitors to their own lands. And scattered along the way there are deflating concessions to the miserable situation: 'Give to Caesar what is Caesar's ...,' 'Pay tax to whom tax is due.'[22]

There is a fascinating tale in which some serious looking men arrive asking the merry band to pay the temple tax. 'Surely,' the Messiah jests, 'we should be taxing the foreign occupiers, since they've made themselves so at home ... but we don't want to offend these fellows.' And so a coin is then wondrously found in the mouth of a fish, caught in the lake. Pure *bios* from the mouth of pure *zoe*.[23]

*

The first vision above is of the daring and precarious leap from the deathly economies of the powers that be, over to the work of transfiguring life. This move is rash because the giant extractive economies take nearly all the oxygen in the room. The second vision is of patient coexistence with deathly economies; a concession to the present age, where we give those powers what we must for a time, until the opportune moment. The dispiriting discovery of any revolution is that we are more deeply rooted in the present order of things than we know. The exodus is nearly always gradual. There is a savviness between the wisdom of patience and the bravery to jump. Messianic savvy calls on a little of both, every day.

*

Messianic savvy is discerned and cultivated in a togetherness: in *koinonia*. This Greek word connotes both friendship and also partnership. Wherever there is a web of relationships that share a sounding toward transfigured life, there is greater possibility, common abundance, shared wisdom and vision and mutual support. The risk of making the jump is mitigated by a web of relations that support the rash endeavour. Exodus is a task for conspirators. The messianic leap from Herod's workforce to that joyous carnival of feasting, healing and story-telling in the commons was only possible because of the *koinonia* of women in the network.[24] On the other hand, support and solidarity, while bearing and outlasting the grind of the present situation, comes from the same mutuality. *Koinonia* is the spirit of the incremental exodus. Wealth creation alienates; but *koinonia* is the yeast of a better economy, the holding structure of transfiguring work.

*

'It's easier to imagine the end of the world than to imagine the end of capitalism.'[25] Interestingly, this famous saying is more or less equally true of the advocates of capitalism and its opponents. The beneficiaries say there is no alternative. The discontented see capitalism as a tyranny from which there is no outside. The brilliant economics podcaster Della Duncan once said that, actually, we all live in many different economies at once: gift economies, skill sharing economies, welfare, economies of friendship and reciprocity, voluntary economies, charitable economies, huge economies of unpaid labour, which are mostly 'manned' by women.[26] Work is much more than employment or jobs. There's richness in the complexity. I feel a little less stuck in that eternal capitalist *now*, when I turn my attention to that richness. I begin to see what I want to lean into, what I want to move out of, and what I will patiently bear with for a time.

*

I learned from the artist Lydia Catterall how to create abundance maps by hosting gatherings in which people from a particular locality would explore together what they have, what they need and where they resonate, so that, between them, they can begin to jigsaw together and find abundance in even their small complexity. With knowing one another comes the possibility of meeting one another's needs and supporting one another's endeavours. A faithfully lived *koinonia* is a small economy. It maps together and moves together toward transfiguring work. It's a sacred space where the *nomos* of capitalist work – of wealth creation versus scarcity – is suspended, and the truth of a forgotten abundance is revealed.

*

Beneath the numbing smog of wealth creation is the small and beautiful work in places, enacted by bodies, with love, toward life transfigured. It is a movement from everywhere to here, from chains of command to relationships of friendship and reciprocity; from quantitative to qualitative; from job to craft, or task or care. Here, everything moves toward a different scale, where care and conviviality are not only possible but also natural. Here is a space fitting for the dance.

Craft, Cultivation and Smallness

About halfway through our symposium on craft, I realized I had no interest in defining the term itself. I want to be in a world full of craft, but I felt as if I would do violence to that deep wanting by trying to overly define it. Perhaps it's because craft exists so deeply in the particular. The virtues, rules and specificities of one craft may overlap with another, but I doubt that it's ever entirely the same and I doubt that it should be. I feel quite sure that craft should not be managed from above but, rather, should be crafted itself by the immediate relations, traditions and provocations on the ground.

Since all this led to questions about the broader realm of work, I found myself wishing that all work was craft of some shade, perhaps alongside its organic sibling: cultivation. We craft or cultivate our children's formative experiences, fresh tomatoes, wisely formed dwellings, loose manifestos and protocols, safe localities, friendship with animals, learning spaces, parties, furniture, healing practices, good paper, fireside stories and generative ideas. Craft and cultivation suggest work on the scale of the particular, with attention to relationship, care and excellence. At the scale of craft and cultivation, our work is transfigured by its own nature.

*

The priest and author Azariah France Williams said the following things at our gathering on craft, which I relay at the end of this sketch of ideas to locate it in the longer tale.

'Work that liberates', he said, 'will be taxed and co-opted by law and power.' The roads wind, fork, intersect and fork again. After the mountains, as the proverb says, there are more mountains.

'Work is formed using templates and traditions from the past, but will transgress and move beyond them.' Our own work re-forms those templates into shapes that others will, and must, transgress. 'The grass will grow over what we make,' says Azariah.

This describes something of the gentleness and violence of eschatological craft. How to live the complexity of such a path well and peacefully?

Azariah's last question stays with me as the beginning point for hopeful work: 'With whom are you unmaking yesterday, to remake today for the benefit of tomorrow?' What kind of social relations – from friendship, to community, to economic agreements – make good craft and cultivation the common stuff of a shared life? Where, for you, is the *koinonia* that enables transfiguring work?

*

As the means, so the ends. With work, as with all things, the *telos* must remain wild, beyond the control or totalizing knowledge claims of any party. It's over the horizon. It is to be gently held by faith in something beyond our holding. Blessed unknowing and wondrous anticipation, good work and good friends all the way.

Notes

1. See Romans 8.20.
2. Ruskin, *Unto This Last and Other Writings*, p. 222.
3. '[If] the God that the Puritan sees as acting in all fortunes of life reveals to one of his children the opportunity to make a profit, then there is a purpose in this. Consequently, the believing Christian must follow this call by taking advantage of this opportunity. If God show you a way in which you may lawfully *get more* than in another way (without wrong to your soul or to any other), if you refuse this and choose the less gainful way, *you cross one of the ends of your calling, and you refuse to be God's steward*' (Weber, *The Protestant Ethic and the 'Spirit' of Capitalism and Other Writings*, p. 110, emphasis added). Weber is quoting the Puritan minister Richard Baxter. See *The Protestant Ethic*, pp. 105–22.
4. *Telos*, Greek for 'ends', 'terminus' or 'destination'.
5. Morris, *Useful Work Versus Useless Toil*, pp. 10–19.
6. Lewis and Maslin, *The Human Planet*, p. 318.
7. The reason the colonization of the Americas caused a dip in atmospheric carbon dioxide (rather than a spike, as in the present predicament), is that upwards of 130 million indigenous Americans died over the course of two centuries, which led to massive forest regrowth and a hundred years of global cooling.
8. See Matthew 17.
9. See John 10.10.
10. Kimmerer, *The Democracy of Species*, p. 14.
11. Kimmerer, *Democracy of Species*, p. 15.
12. Romans 8.20.
13. Raworth, *Doughnut Economics*, pp. 35–57.
14. See Romans 13.8–10.
15. See Ephesians 2.8–10.
16. See James 3.14–17.
17. See John 16.33.
18. Sacks, *The Dignity of Difference*, p. 56.
19. 'Is not this the carpenter, the son of Mary?' (Mark 6.3). The word is *tekton*, which means 'carpenter', 'joiner' or 'builder'.
20. See Luke 8.1–3.
21. See Luke 2.1.
22. See Mark 12.17; Romans 13.7.
23. See Matthew 17.24–27.
24. See Luke 8.1–3.
25. This quotation is attributed to both Frederic Jameson and Slavoj Žižek in Mark Fisher's book *Capitalist Realism*, p. 2.
26. Della Duncan can be found on the *Upstream* podcast, http://www.upstreampodcast.org.

7

The Sacred Absence of Rule

A while ago, a good friend found himself expecting two new souls to join him in his work. They would be a team, and the new arrivals would be, as we say, working under him. He asked around for any thoughts on non-hierarchical ways of approaching such things. Another good friend, who will never waste an opportunity for a symposium, set up a series of discussions playfully titled *Hieranarchy*. And so we gathered to explore the questions. What are we really doing when we build a world of hierarchies around ourselves? Why do we do nearly everything this way? What would it mean to stop, and how would we cease our compulsive remaking of this same old world again and again?

Objections to these flaneuring inquiries into how the world is arranged usually come down to some jeering questions. Do you have a better idea? What is the alternative? I think these are trick questions. I'll not rise to them. I'm not foolish enough to suggest, or even clever enough to dream up, an alternative structure to our blessed and immutable hierarchies. I sense that any attempt to dream up an alternative structure would leave us in at least half the same problems and another set of new ones. What I believe we can do is explore practices, virtues and behaviours that would loosen our desperate reliance on hierarchies and create the space and the conditions for strange and wonderful new things to happen. As it is said, the rainmaker doesn't cause the rain, she simply allows it to happen.

THE MESSIANIC COMMONS

Ways of Seeing Power

I am fascinated by how quick we are to accept hierarchies as an inescapable reality, with no outside. It's easier to imagine the end of the world than it is to imagine the end of capitalism,[1] so we just explore how capitalism might be done a little differently. We take a similar approach to our hierarchies.

A vertical chain of command. A pyramidal power structure. The etymological roots take us to phrases such as 'sacred rule', and I think, in this case, 'sacredness' is very much conditioned to imply not otherness but straightforward vertical superiority: rule from above.

*

The reality that power exists and is exercised is often taken as evidence of the encompassing isness of hierarchies. Hierarchies exist because power exists. They're believed to be one and the same thing, just the way things are. If this is so, then the only question is how to do them better or more benevolently.

A while ago, I asked a friend who is part of the Hualapai tribe in Arizona to describe Hualapai spirituality to me. He began by saying that before there was a god, there was power: energy, or life, if you will. Power permeates everything. One may hold a different creation myth, but the Pai account helps us to recognize the obvious thing: that power *is*, and power precedes the human world and its structures. Looking at how power, energy, life and purpose seem to exist and behave in the biosphere might be a good exercise. Perhaps we will find that the existence of power and our arrangement of it into hierarchies are not one and the same thing. Perhaps ecology can show us alternative visions of how to dance with power.

*

'Power' is not to be found in the etymology of hierarchy. The Greek word *archo* means rule. Rule doesn't mean power; it describes the authority to wield it.

*

A gentler definition of hierarchy might be something such as *ordering power* but, even so, a problem remains; a conceit, even. Robin Wall Kimmerer describes how her native language reserves the impersonal pronoun 'it' for human-made things only. Trees, stones and stars will have a personal pronoun.[2] The polar opposite would be the Modernity world view that sees nature as other, as an 'it', and as inanimate stuff to be carved up and used by humans, the dominant species. When we speak of ordering power, or structuring it, we operate within this European colonial assumption about the world. We talk about power as a resource; as a *stuff*. What if we didn't talk about ordering power as though it were a stuff to be used, but rather interacting or dancing with power as an immersive reality in which we're participants? We would then think in terms of how we position ourselves, within an ecological whole, of which we are part. Our endeavours would be integrated and open and adaptable in character, rather than closed and mechanistic. I suspect rigid hierarchies would become very difficult from the ground of this imagination.

*

Those two Greek words come to us once again: *bios* exists and is held within *zoe*. Wise forms of *bios* exist in a reciprocal dance with *zoe*.

*

At school, my children learn competition. They find themselves vertically ranked according to their ability to reproduce what their superiors have banked in them. They are obliged to learn the arts of equilibrium elsewhere. They are primed by the state toward competitive, linear and vertical thinking.

*

Hierarchies make all human relationships binary: one is higher and the other is lower.

*

THE MESSIANIC COMMONS

While listening to our discussion on hierarchies, I kept wondering about the structures those human relations exist in. We may have a hierarchical ladder or pyramid of human power relations, but within what? A business? An organization? A clique? A church? A state? And to what end? What is the purpose of that body? For what task does it exist? Can the purpose change or is it set? It would seem that the person at the top of the hierarchy is the most powerless to question the purpose of the machine they run. It is their job to preserve the running order of the machine. They are usually its most rigidly loyal servants. I recall hearing stories about bankers wanting to change the culture of the organism they worked in, but, in spite of their wealth and privilege, they always found themselves powerless to make any mark on the creature. There is more freedom from this grip the lower down the pyramid we go, though there is also less power to act on it.

Thus creativity becomes an imperative at the bottom. Creative pursuits are systemically untethered. Plato's warning to the rulers was quite true: if you set artists free, they will destroy your orderly arrangements.

*

Hierarchy is the internal structure that powers and principalities use to preserve themselves against change. It is a structure that maximizes the efficiency of the machine, and minimizes its need to alter itself amid the flux of *zoe* and the winds of change. It boundaries and ossifies.

*

God enters temples with a wary eye. It is known that we sometimes build temples to contain and ossify God. God prefers the fluid architecture of the tent. The tent is the architecture of the sacred imagination.

*

The vertical imagination of the tower of Babel correlates with its singular, unshifting vision. God's answer to such linear dullness is to mix up language, so the upward building project comes to a halt: instead, there is a multitude of diverging dialects for horizontal networks of life. God plays the trickster figure. God disturbs the water. It is, of course, not the tower that God destroys but the structure of relations that enables a chain of command in the service of a singular vision or purpose. The tower remains. It is retaken by *zoe*: by the trees, the vines and the birds.

*

Hierarchy is a system of borders, a collection of laws, a *nomos*. It is a law that is external to individuals and that manages their power relations for them. It is either written in the company handbook or worn into the cultural imagination as a passively received awareness of whose voice carries most weight.

*

Years ago, I was a team leader in a mission organization. We were supposed to give Bible studies to university student leaders, as they were called, who would then do the Bible studies with other students. Instead of handing them questions, I hosted spaces where the student leaders could explore the texts and propose their own questions. For this, I was demoted from the job and put behind a desk. What was the problem? The problem was that they who set the questions have power: the power to shift the structure's vision and purpose. The power to set the questions was not allowed to fall down to the bottom half of the pyramid.

Every time I was pushed out of a hierarchical structure (I am certainly not an impartial commentator here), it wasn't because I questioned who had the power but because I questioned what the structure itself was trying to do. This has been exactly the same in both conservative and progressive spheres. My clashing with the hierarchy tended to emerge from my questions because, as I slowly learned, I wasn't high enough up the chain of command to ask those questions. Nor was anyone who asked such questions allowed up the chain of command. My issue was never first and foremost about hierarchical structures, but about what we were doing and why we were doing

THE MESSIANIC COMMONS

it. Hierarchy became a question for me because I commonly experienced it as a system that defended the structure against my questions. Many times, hierarchy has come to me as a structural defence against change and the flux of life.

*

We can decentre power, but it's much harder to decentre the power to decentre power. It's much easier to give away from our stores (if we have them) than it is to alter the fact that we have stores to give away from. Power relations have roots that go back in time where we can't reach them. Hierarchies are not only to be understood as pyramids of power at work in the present, but also as genealogies of power that hold a structural integrity through time. It is acts of a sort of magical, creative bravery that alter the course that power takes into the future.

*

So, a pyramid of hierarchical human relations exists among a group of people bound together within the circle of a common purpose. They are an organization, a business, a church, a club or what have you – a collection of people with various roles and positions of importance in a common endeavour. That circle exists within the general malaise of *bios*, of life as we humans have constructed it around ourselves in various forms: capitalism, democracy, religion, social norms and so on. This realm of *bios* exists within the bigger circle of *zoe*, the ecological whole, the greater realm of the living planet. Hierarchies are the spine of managed social relations that uphold ordered, controlled and boundaried checkpoints between these concentric circles. A hierarchy exists to acquire and hold power within its walls, from all that is without. It gathers power into the business, the organization, the club or the state and holds onto it. Similarly, the *bios* of the human realm has tended toward acquiring and holding power for itself from the broader flux of *zoe*, the ecological whole. The human world of *bios* exists as an embattled island within *zoe*. It gradually expands outward, subsuming *zoe* into itself.

THE SACRED ABSENCE OF RULE

In this vision, we've arranged our life in the world as a castle that has a series of concentric circular walls. This is the unspoken purpose of all hierarchies. Alternative approaches to power will move across these borders, making them porous and shaking these concentric circles into a more interconnected complex. From here, we might begin to imagine visions where power is not enclosed but given to its natural flow; where the one who leads continually changes, depending on the task. There is change all the time. The purpose of the broader body or group develops according to what is happening. The plot is alive to what wants to happen in relation to the people on board and the changing reality in the greater realm of *bios*, which is shifting in relation to the even greater realm *zoe*. Improvisation and dance are allowed to happen.

*

The word *hieranarchy* was made up in jest by my friend Paul Milbank. I like it more all the time. We might translate it as *the sacred absence of rule*. 'He has abolished the law,' so it says.[3] The word 'abolished' is *katargesas*, which means to 'suspend', 'to render inoperative' or, perhaps, 'to ossify'. The Messiah does to law exactly what law does to the world. The New Testament answer to the absence of law is not lawlessness but spirit, *pneuma*, breath. The sacred absence of ossifying rule is filled instead with the endless life-giving movement of breath.

Towers of Babel and Factory Farms

Why do those who languish at the bottom of hierarchies accept them, since they are the more numerous and, in the sense described above, freer of them? What do they get out of this structure? At the top of the tower, it's easy to see how the lovers of control and order, efficiency, growth and conquest are well served. Meanwhile, at the bottom, there is a correlating drive for security and for a holding structure that is predictable and reliable. As the philosopher Thomas Hobbes said, we accept the tyranny of the sovereign over us because the sovereign keeps us safe.[4] We submit to the wisdom that a hierarchy is necessary and in our best interests because it's the rulers who keep chaos and deathly disorder at bay. The hierarchy says to those on the lowest rungs, *don't bite the hand that feeds.*

There is an ambiguity at play when we rail against our political powers by saying (as we did during the coronavirus pandemic): 'You have failed to keep us safe.' When we say this, we might be saying one of two different things. We might be saying, *the promises of hierarchical human life are false. Let's rethink how we live.* Conversely, we might be saying, *we have to re-establish the functionality of this hierarchy.* In the latter case, we are not questioning the hierarchical structure but deferring to it, and demanding that those at the top fulfil their mythic obligations to keep us safe. We fear, or perhaps cannot even imagine, having responsibility for our own life together.

This leads to questions about human nature, if there is any one such thing. Hobbes' view was based on the belief that human life is characterized by the war of every man against every man.[5] Human life is fundamentally selfish and violent, and must be managed from above in order to save it from destroying itself. Protestant theology prefigured Hobbes' view in its descriptions of the human as universally and totally depraved.

*

Beside this estimation of human depravity is a view of nature as chaos. Between this rock and a hard place, a space of managed order must be kept against the chaos without and over the chaos within. The human realm of *bios* forces out a space of order amid the chaos of *zoe*. The more developed a civilization was, the closer to God. The indigenous peoples of colonized lands who lived entwined in their environmental rhythms were commonly understood to be savage, less than fully human, and in league with devilish spiritual powers.

At the back door of Modernity, the more-than-human world reappears, not as a chaos to be pillaged but as an unmanaged complexity, an astonishingly abundant balance on which we rely completely. Unmanaged complexity is not the same thing as chaos. Today, chaos is the result of managed power convulsing against its edges and constraints. Ecology exercises faith in unmanaged complexity. To bring this principle, or perhaps this faith, into human ecology changes the dance. Relinquishment of a structure that claims to protect us from chaos involves a willingness to move toward what seems chaotic to left-brained Modernity: a faithful letting go of control.

*

Attempts to think outside the principles of hierarchy have tended toward the language of flat structures. Sometimes this language sounds like the ideal vision of a non-hierarchical world. At other times, it sounds more like an attempt to find a balance or a corrective energy amid the hierarchies we can't realistically escape.

A friend told a story. She was leading an organization that had an apparently flat structure. Her common experience was that her propositions never flew, and the ones that did always came from the same few men. So she exercised the hierarchical potential of her role as the leader to address that continual deference to the rule of male voices.

It's a common observation that flat structures may just lead to the rule of the loudest voices and the most privileged platforms. Here, the structure of hierarchy was being used to dismantle that tendency.

There are hierarchies overlaid on hierarchies. Organizational hierarchies exist within the implicit and unwritten hierarchies of the social whole; there are covert genealogical power structures that go back into histories of power and privilege. They are all the more pernicious because they are unwritten and undeclared. The written law and the unwritten law; hierarchies, both solid and ghostly. It's hard to unmake one without unmaking the other. The same groups generally prevail in both kinds. We may even find ourselves obliged to use one as a defence against the tyranny of the other.

Correspondingly, the working association of people who relate to one another in a fluid human ecology that dances with power in wise improvisation will correlate to a change in world view, from anthropocentric Modernity toward an ecology of *all our relations*.

*

If hierarchies sound like towers of Babel, flat structures sound like factory farms. They might both be ways of managing the movements of people into a desired order. They might both assume an association of people with a fixed purpose. They may both seek shortcuts to virtue, as they see it, with enforced boundaries. They both sound like ways of managing the absence of relationships that are good enough to trust.

When a group shifts to a flat structure, the measure of success is often that it's as efficient as it ever was as a hierarchy. Perhaps even more so. But until the make-up of the collective has become something with the self-awareness to collectively ask what it is even doing and why, and to change its course, the grind of despoiling progress continues, only by friendlier means.

There are two questions, then. First, how to form better places to be, to live and to work together? The second, deeper question is, how can these become spaces in which work can be reimagined and reconfigured? A flat structure might just be one stage in that bigger process. Or it might be a way of staving off the deeper change that wants to happen, such as trying to fix climate change with carbon capture technology so we don't have to rethink our abusive and extractive relationship with our ecological whole.

To put it differently, hierarchies are an answer to the question *what kind of human relations do we need, to get our things done?* I think we need to flip the question around to this: *what do we need to do to engender the best possible human, and more-than-human, relations?* My issue with flat structures, or indeed other kinds of reform, is that they often answer the first question, not the second.

*

If not flat structures, then what? I am compelled by the language of hosting. Healthy movement in human relations between hosting and guesting creates space for more emergent possibilities. Andy Knox spoke a fascinating thing into the symposium: he said that hierarchies can be dismantled from within by people forming strong relationships across boundaries of difference. Why? What new thing does this intentional practice make possible?

*

'All our relations,' say the Lakota, whenever they enter or leave the sweat lodge to pray. All our relations, meaning, all people, animals, plants, trees, rocks, rivers, mountains, suns and galaxies.[6] These words ground us in relation to all things. I'm feeling toward the kinds of collaborative relations that are in harmony with this brief prayer. What does it look like to hold a relational space of endeavour, where the relationships can be trusted and don't have to be managed and separated out by internal law? What does it look like to trust what emerges amid good relationships, and then have the courage to alter the course taken?

Trickery and Reversals

In the Gospel stories, the messianic posture toward hierarchies is always that of the trickster. The Messiah playfully reverses roles and messes with status markers wherever pyramids of power are to be found. The first will be last, and the last will be first.[7] Yes, John is the greatest, but the least of us is greater than John.[8] Go for the cheap seats and land in the royal box. Go for the seat of power and be thrown out with the riff-raff.[9] These reversals of power and position are persistent.

This sits in resonance with Hebrew prophetic tradition and with messianic expectation. Every mountain shall be laid low, and every valley shall be levelled.[10] But we may distinguish between two slightly different energies here. The laying low and the levelling up have a sense of justice between parties divided by woeful inequalities, and also a messianic sense of completion: the world's contradictions resolved and at rest. The Messiah of the Gospels, on the other hand, does not resolve the world's contradictions, but perplexes them with trickery, mockery and reversal. He is very much in the tensions of the moment, unmasking them. He is in the messy middle, not at the serene end. He actually appears to be making things worse by upsetting what little equilibrium we have managed to conjure with our various power structures. This too sits in the Hebrew tradition that brings the proud low and lifts up the downcast – but not before the proud have them double the quota of bricks. Mary's song sings in the same disruptive key: the low are lifted up and the rich are introduced to food poverty.[11]

*

The messianic taboo of the New Testament is that even God's image is not spared from this strangeness. In this Messiah, Word becomes flesh, the ageless becomes the newborn, the judge becomes the convict, the sovereign power becomes the homeless wanderer.

*

There's been a tendency in my circles to view these reversals as images of the last things: how it will finally be when everything is one day made new. Then the first shall be last. Then the last shall be first. Then, but not now. The messianic figure, on the other hand, doesn't just go around making pronouncements. He embodies and enacts the trickery of reversals. Perhaps we might be awoken to new possibilities if we saw this principle not just as the ends but also as the means. Here is a messianic praxis of subverting hierarchies.

I carry a growing suspicion of the theological language of 'announcements'. The Messiah announces the kingdom, the jubilee, the great reversal. Why the suspicion? Because, so often, even those who peddle those 'announcements' embody no such thing. Very little trickery reaches these towering institutions and their powerful figures, who talk as though they have answers. The language of announcements has become just one more way that all great reversals are forever kicked down the road. By keeping the messianic language of reversals locked away in the age to come, the powerful seem almost better able to hold on to their present power. They assure everyone that all will be arighted in the end. We can even lay claim to the virtue of such announcements by merely announcing them. Such is the Jewish critique of a toothless Christian messianism, where everything is said to be different and nothing is actually different at all.

What does this messianic practice of subverting hierarchies achieve if it is practised now, in the broken middle of the story, and not just passively projected on to its end? It is a practice that liberates life from *nomos*. It liberates *zoe* from *bios*, and *bios* from itself. It restores the free movement of power from its captivity to the powerful and its forced exclusion from the powerless. It awakens that which is ossified in bounded structures to soft, vulnerable, living tissue again.

*

The US theologian Dr Willie Jennings spoke about segregation as a structure that separates people into groups living in siloed ignorance of others' lives. This, he said, was about control. Through the messianic practice of subverting hierarchies, the Messiah abolishes the dividing wall that segregates one group from another. This practice destroys the control that holds the world together in its present form.[12]

This sacred language of reversals is not a voice of generic discontent, but a practice to be embodied and lived out in transgressive acts against the boundaries that ossify power and freeze the living ecology of all things.

*

Who are these great leaders, Peter, Paul, Silas or anyone else? 'All things belong to you,' says Paul. 'No more boasting about men,' he adds.[13] Paul makes jibes against the Corinthians' deference to hierarchies, and the patronage of the powerful. Why? Because he envisages all things as a complex of relations between all: all our relations. The phrase 'all things' appears more often in this letter than any other. Paul sees no gatekeepers, no tiers, no walls within walls. The concentric circles are banished by the mere refusal to recognize them. All have direct access to all things, as members of all things and participants in the life of all things. No mediators. All of us, in relation to all our relations.

In this letter, Paul's blasé dismissal of all hierarchies is striking in contrast to the cautious tinkering we're used to seeing. How can he so carelessly walk around the demon that has so many of us totally enthralled? One distinction is that we try to address the problem of hierarchy from wholly within *bios*. It's a human structure to be replaced with a human structure, if only we could come up with something that would work. To Paul, this makes no sense from the outset because he sees structures of *bios* within the greater context of *zoe*: the more-than-human world. His political theology has a much overlooked indigeneity to it. From this standpoint, hierarchies seem as foolish to Paul as legal land ownership does to many indigenous peoples.

We see Paul challenging the pernicious hierarchical imagination at the dinner table.[14] He breaks up divisions between economic classes and between masters and slaves as they sit for the ritualized breaking of bread. It would be better not to participate than to do so in a setting of hierarchical law. To mix these together is to show that you have no idea what you are participating in.

Paulos writes much about table manners. When people of difference are gathered to eat together, how can they connect as interdependent relations across the social markers that distinguish one group from another? What kind of awareness, sensitivity, acceptance and generosity must be developed in order to form a living *koinonia* across boundaries of law, belonging and experience? Paul gives much energy to the work of exploring the art of hosting and guesting across boundaries. Why? Because this art will be the basis of the kind of *koinonia* from which the faithful shared endeavour might emerge, without recourse to hierarchies. He awakens the virtues from which abundance may emerge out of unmanaged complexity.

THE SACRED ABSENCE OF RULE

Hosting and Guesting

Practise hospitality. Welcome strangers. In doing so we may unwittingly find ourselves entertaining angels.[15] We may even be hosting the disguised Messiah.[16] Host anyone, by all means, but especially strangers and others. Host those outside your own circle. Host those beneath your circle. Host those who exist on a different tier of ossified hierarchical power. When we do, that power experiences a small liberation. This is a small exodus of power from its captivity to one tier of the hierarchy, from its domestication by the anxious interests that freeze the world solid.

*

When we host those among our own group, we may hardly be hosting at all. We might only be mutually wandering around a palace of mirrors. When we host the other, we host the messianic.

And yet only with some artfulness can we say that the Messiah hosts. The New Testament Messiah never hosts in the straightforward sense. 'The whole earth is mine,' says the God of the Hebrews.[17] And yet the Messiah wanders around it homeless. The Messiah has no doorway to welcome anyone through and no table to gather anyone around. The Messiah is the serial guest, in one house after another: the house of the Pharisee, the tax collector, the leper and the fisherman's mother-in-law. It's natural enough to imagine Messiahs atop all imagined hierarchies; but messianic life journeys downward, becoming a guest to everyone until finally falling beneath all hierarchies.

So, while we are hosts, we host the messianic. But while we are guests, we are embodying messianic space.

*

There is a power relation between host and guest. The host has the greater power. The guest has less.

I remember, as a child, reading one of Aesop's fables, in which the fox invites the stork to dinner and serves up soup in shallow bowls. The fox laps it up with his tongue while the stork is at a loss, with his long beak, and goes hungry. Then, later, the stork invites the fox and serves up soup in tall thin vases. He reaches his long beak into the vase and drinks the soup, while the fox can't get anywhere near it. The guest is always subject to the greater power of the host.

Here's a more beautiful vision: the host makes space for the guest to bring their whole self, knowing that the guest carries a messianic gift that the host needs in order to be liberated and come alive. Then, some days later, the host journeys to the place where the guest lives and sits at their table. The host is now the guest, and experiences the messianic powerlessness of being subject to another's hospitality and the jarring different rhythms of their world. The one who now hosts makes space for their guest to bring their whole self and receives the strange gift that their otherness brings. Power is stuck nowhere. Power is in movement everywhere. The dividing boundaries are broken down in the fluid movement of hosting and guesting.

*

Here, then, is a vision of how we might approach power, order, endeavour and relationship differently. Rule and law, of which hierarchies are a kind, exist to make up for a deficit of relationships and good faith. The thinner the relationship, the more law is deemed necessary. The more law binds power, the more the virtues of relationship and good faith wither. Eventually, a functioning human ecology based on relationship and good faith becomes unimaginable and apparently unworkable. All must be policed and managed by law, by the concentric walls and gates of so many hierarchies. The intentional practice of guesting and hosting gently unmakes hierarchical boundaries and binaries, while at the same time cultivating an alternative human ecology of fruitful, faithful relationships.

This relational human ecology reaches toward the wisdom of unmanaged complexity seen amid all our relations. Here is the practice of faith in God's *sofia*, God's wisdom, as we encounter her in the unmanaged complexity of the ecological whole. We participate by a relenting. We refrain from imposing controlling law upon the world. Instead we exercise relational virtues that engender healthy relationships. Thus, something such as *pneuma* guides the movement of our shared endeavours, and not law. Let's call it *the sacred absence of rule.*

*

What does this mean? It means we cannot significantly alter our hierarchical structures without fundamentally altering the shape and vision of the whole thing, from nation state, to business, to book club. What it *is*, what it is *here for*, and what its *ends* shall be must all break open to change. We would need to exchange efficiency for truth. We would be exchanging embattled growth for a dance of balance. We would exchange our water-tight ships for fluidity itself. We would exchange power and strength for peaceableness and laughter. We would be relinquishing the assumed goals of empires: permanence, dominion and assured satisfaction. We would instead adopt the nomadic posture, accepting all things and all places as gift, beyond all fictions of exclusive ownership.

*

Without a transformation of our relationship to everything – the very fabric of all our human associations and endeavours – we can only tinker with our hierarchies. It is a part of the great and dreadful everything-task which is growing before the world. But there is something that is not to be done. It is no one's task to create an ingenious alternative structure and artfully roll it into the gap left by our abandoned hierarchies. No one is now asked to repeat the old mistake and make the faithless assumption that *zoe* must be managed from above.

Rather than roll out a new structure to replace the old, we instead begin to practise a new behaviour that alters the conditions of our human ecology: the radical messianic practice of guesting and hosting across boundaries of difference. This practice places faith in the unmanaged complexity of all things. It places faith in *sofia*, as she is amid the earth and the world. In this faith, our hierarchies naturally become something different in accordance with the wisdom that emerges from reconnection to one another and to all our relations. We re-situate ourselves, in faith, amid the unmanaged complexity.

*

The practice of guesting and hosting is an art, a wisdom and a virtue. Aesop reminds us to beware of the counterfeit. It is quite possible to be a host or a guest without art, wisdom or virtue. There's nothing messianic about this.

*

Being formed in the messianic practice of guesting and hosting, the individual lets down their defensive structures and enters deeper into joyous, peaceable relationship to All Things. They find themselves in gentle movement, having nothing yet possessing everything.

Similarly, the group journeying together – the business, the institution or the collective – becomes fluid, porous and versatile, at peace with the flux of their endeavour and the flux without. They're even at peace with the end of the endeavour because their relation to all things cannot end. Whether a book club or a nation state, all structures are warmed to softness, aliveness and change.

Here lies a vision in which the whole realm of *bios* is softened. Its walls are lowered and it loosens its grasping and adversarial relationship to *zoe*. First, it begins to host *zoe* as guest and to receive her gifts. Then it recognizes itself, finally, as *zoe's* guest, which is the truer vision of things. From here, a wisened dance begins to emerge on the basis of a porous relationship of faith and balance between *bios* and *zoe*. An unmanaged complexity centred on good relations is free to emerge amid the sacred absence of rule.

*

Gershom Scholem describes messianism as 'the anarchic breeze'. Why? Because when the Messiah comes and heals the world there will be no law, no *nomos*. The world will no longer require rule of any kind to keep it from slipping into disaster. This vision is associated with the age to come. Law and rule is

THE SACRED ABSENCE OF RULE

associated with the present age. The sacredness or holiness of the absence of rule lies in its otherness to the rule of the present age. The absence of rule is holy. The absence of rule is sacred. The absence of rule is other. The messianism that emerged in the first century was described as a way, and the way was something like this: to embody the sacred absence of rule today, and to allow the consequences to play out into what will be.

Notes

1 A saying attributed to both Frederic Jameson and Slavoj Žižek. See Fisher, *Capitalist Realism*, p. 2.

2 Robin Wall Kimmerer, interviewed by Krista Tippett, 'The Intelligence of Plants', *On Being* [podcast], E1060, originally aired 25 February 2016, updated 12 May 2022, https://onbeing.org/programs/robin-wall-kimmerer-the-intelligence-of-plants-2022 (accessed 3.10.2024).

3 Ephesians 2.15.

4 'Hereby it is manifest, that during the time men live without a common Power to keep them all in awe, they are in that condition which is called Warre; and such a warre, as is of every man, against every man. For WARRE, consisteth not in Battell onely, or the act of fighting; but in a tract of time, wherein the Will to contend by Battell is sufficiently known: and therefore the notion of *Time*, is to be considered in the nature of Warre' (Hobbes, *Leviathan*, p. 88).

5 Hobbes, *Leviathan*, p. 88.

6 Fox, *Creation Spirituality*, pp. 7–8.

7 See Matthew 20.16.

8 See Matthew 11.11.

9 See Luke 14.7–14.

10 See Isaiah 40.4.

11 See Luke 1.41–53.

12 Dr Jennings, speaking at a Neighbourhood Economics event, 17 November 2020. A recording of his talk is available at 'Faith + Finance Neighbourhood Economics Virtual Conference' [video], YouTube, 19 November 2020, https://www.youtube.com/watch?v=_-W14u9gwx4 (accessed 18.10.2024).

13 See 1 Corinthians 3.21–22.

14 See 1 Corinthians 11:17–22.

15 See Hebrews 13.2.

16 See Matthew 25.31–46.

17 See Psalm 50.12.

Bibliography

Adorno, Theodor, 2005, *Minima Moralia*, London: Verso.
Agamben, Giorgio, 1998, *Homo Sacer*, Stanford, CA: Stanford University Press.
―― 2004, *The Open*, Stanford, CA: Stanford University Press.
―― 2005, *State of Exception*, London and Chicago, IL: Chicago University Press.
Benjamin, Walter, 1992, *Illuminations*, London: Fontana Press.
―― 2007, *Reflections*, New York: Schocken.
Berger, Peter L. and Luckmann, Thomas, 1985, *The Social Construction of Reality*, London: Penguin.
Berry, Wendell, 2021, *What I Stand For Is What I Stand On*, London: Penguin.
Bonhoeffer, Dietrich, 1966, *Letters and Papers from Prison*, London: Fontana.
Brewin, Kester, 2012, *Mutiny!*, London: Vaux.
Bruce, F. F., 1983, *The Gospel of John*, Grand Rapids, MI: Eerdmans.
Buber, Martin, 1951, *Two Types of Faith*, London: Routledge & Paul.
Cavanaugh, William T., 2002, *Theopolitical Imagination*, London/New York: Bloomsbury.
Cayley, David, 2005, *Rivers North of the Future*, Toronto: House of Anansi.
Cohen, Abraham, 1995, *Everyman's Talmud*, New York: Schocken.
Eusebius, 1967, *The History of the Church from Christ to Constantine*, London: Penguin.
Ewell III, Samuel E., 2020, *Faith Seeking Conviviality*, Eugene, OR: Cascade.
Federici, Silvia, 2021, *Caliban and the Witch*, London: Penguin.
Fisher, Mark, 2009, *Capitalist Realism*, Winchester: Zero Books.
Fox, Matthew, 1991, *Creation Spirituality*, San Francisco, CA: Harper.
Grey, Mary C., 2003, *Sacred Longings*, London: SCM Press.
Hine, Dougald, 2023, *At Work in the Ruins*, London: Chelsea Green.
Hobbes, Thomas, 1997, *Leviathan*, Cambridge: Cambridge University Press.
Julian of Norwich, 1966, *Revelations of Divine Love*, London: Penguin.

BIBLIOGRAPHY

Kimmerer, Robin Wall, 2021, *The Democracy of Species*, London: Penguin.
Lewis, Simon, L. and Maslin, Mark A., 2018, *The Human Planet*, London: Pelican.
Lowy, Michael, 2016, *Fire Alarm*, London: Verso.
McLuhan, Marshall, 2001, *Understanding Media*, New York: Routledge.
McLuhan, Marshall and Fiore, Quentin, 1997, *War and Peace in the Global Village*, San Francisco, CA: Hardwired.
Malcolm, Hannah (ed.), 2020, *Words for a Dying World*, London: SCM Press.
Meeks, Wayne A., 1983, *The First Urban Christians*, New Haven, CT: Yale University Press.
Merchant, Carolyn, '"The Violence of Impediments": Francis Bacon and the Origins of Experimentation', *Isis* 99:4 (December 2008), pp. 731–60.
Miller, Lee, 1997, *From the Heart: Voices of the American Indian*, London: Pimlico.
Morris, William, 2008, *Useful Work Versus Useless Toil*, London: Penguin.
Myers, Ched, 2008, *Binding the Strongman*, New York: Orbis.
Pascal, Blaise, 1995, *Pensées*, London: Penguin.
Raworth, Kate, 2018, *Doughnut Economics*, London: Penguin.
Ruskin, John, 1997, *Unto This Last and Other Writings*, London: Penguin.
Sacks, Jonathan, 2003, *The Dignity of Difference*, New York/London: Continuum.
Scholem, Gershom, 1995, *The Messianic Idea in Judaism and Other Essays on Jewish Spirituality*, New York: Schocken.
Stearn, Gerald Emanuel (ed.), 1968, *McLuhan Hot & Cool*, London: Penguin.
Taubes, Jacob, 2010, *From Cult to Culture*, Stanford, CA: Stanford University Press.
—— 2009, *Occidental Eschatology*, Stanford, CA: Stanford University Press.
Theodoret, 2010, *Ecclesiastical History*, Whitefish, MT: Kessinger.
Tolkien, J. R. R., 1979, *Tree and Leaf; Smith of Wootton Major; The Homecoming of Beorhtnoth Beorhthelm's Son*, London: Unwin.
Weber, Max, 2002, *The Protestant Ethic and the 'Spirit' of Capitalism and Other Writings*, London: Penguin.
Williams, Rowan, 2021, *Looking East in Winter*, London: Bloomsbury.
Wink, Walter, 1998, *The Powers That Be*, New York: Galilee Doubleday.
Wright, N. T. 2013, *Paul and the Faithfulness of God*, London: SPCK.

www.ingramcontent.com/pod-product-compliance
Lightning Source LLC
Chambersburg PA
CBHW022017290426
44109CB00015B/1208